The Vanishing Generation

The Vanishing Generation

IRENE MUSILLO MITCHELL

THE PAPER HOUSE
PUBLISHING

Copyright © 2024 by Irene Musillo Mitchell

All rights reserved.

No part of this book may be reproduced in any form or by any electronic or mechanical means, including information storage and retrieval systems, without written permission from the author, except for the use of brief quotations in a book review.

Library of Congress Control Number: 2024902047

ISBN 979-8-8691-0389-5

Ebook ISBN 979-8-8691-0388-8

First Edition

Contents

Prologue	1
Part One: Emigration to America	**3**
1. Montevetuso, the City on the Mountaintop	5
2. Journey to the New World	10
3. Mama in America	15
4. Customs and Cuisine	22
5. Mama's Last Years	33
6. Remembering Mama	39
Part Two: My Father Anthon	**45**
7. Young Anton in Montevetuso	47
8. The Dream of a Piano	53
9. Musical Life in New York City	57
10. The Moving Finger	61
Part Three: My Childhood in the Bronx	**71**
11. Eastville Avenue and Life on the City Block	73
12. The World of Fordham Road	86
13. Schooldays	99
14. From the Insular Block to the Wide World	108
15. Commencement, an Ending and a Beginning	116
Part Four: World War II	**121**
16. The Home Front	123
17. War on the Bronx Streets and Kilroy	128
18. The Tragic Cost of Peace	139
Part Five: Letters from Aunt Raffaella	**147**
19. Fate of Family in Italy	149
20. Fascist Youth	154
21. White Widows	159
22. Aunt Raffaella's Death	167
Part Six: The Vanishing Generation	**171**
23. Perspectives on a Mountaintop City	173
24. Eastville Avenue at Twilight	178
Acknowledgments	181
About the Author	183

Prologue

My narrative could well start with the four transporting words, *"Once upon a time,"* for the world my contemporaries and I lived in has well-nigh vanished. We were the children born in the late 1920s and the early 1930s, during the Great Depression. The era of television, the screen, the Internet, virtual reality, and smartphones lay decades in the future. Our observation and interpretation of the world relied solely on the natural human faculties —what we saw, thought, and imagined.

The world unfolded before us, brimming with potential adventures and challenges, as we endured the hardships of the Second World War and shared the anxieties of our parents. We were the children who were meant to be seen but not heard.

We were taught to learn respect and proper behaviors according to the happenings of the moment.

In our era, the concept of teenagers, as a separate class with its own fashions and literature, had yet to take shape. Girls, in the words of Louisa May Alcott, were to simply grow up into "little women," while some boys, aged seventeen or eighteen, already considered themselves men as they left high school in order to help support their families, donning suits and fedoras.

Living on the tranquil, wooded block in the East Bronx, we spoke with a Bronx accent. Our vocabulary was limited and sometimes marred by mispronunciations. Listening to teachers and hosts on the radio, who spoke impeccable English, began our slow psychological removal from the insularity of the city block.

At that time, the social drive toward "college for all" was not a prominent goal. Graduating high school was the norm, though some could not, burdened by the responsibility of supporting their families. My sister and I were among the few women at that time who took the academic course in high school (which also offered the commercial course and the general course), and through the beneficial programs of the great City of New York, were enabled to enroll in a city college.

The children of my era grew into maturity in a world without the aid of the internet immediately at hand, relying solely on common sense and hazarding judgments we could make with the resources at our disposal. Destiny thrust us into the throes of World War II, and through the valiant efforts of the civilian population and the armed forces, we became known as The Greatest Generation.

These pages, featuring Annalisa and her immigrant Italian family, offer a nostalgic look into our moment in history, we, the vanishing generation, the children who played street games and witnessed the sobriety and heroism of World War II.

Part One

Emigration to America

1

Montevetuso, the City on the Mountaintop

IN ITALY, in the region of Basilicata, there is an ancient city atop a mountain, one of Italy's hill cities, which I have given the name Montevetuso. Perched on the mountaintop, it was discovered by the Greeks around the eighth century, B.C. when they colonized it, establishing it as part of Magna Graecia. In the fourth century, B.C., atop of the ruins of the preexisting Greek city, Roman Emperor Alexander Severus established a Roman city, subsequently known as Civitas Severiana. Thus, Montevetuso became part of the Roman Empire.

In the fourth century, A.D., the Roman Empire underwent a division into two halves: the western half, with Rome as its capital, and the eastern half under the Byzantine Empire with Constantinople as its capital. Montevetuso then became part of the Byzantine Empire. In the eleventh century, A.D., the region fell under the rule of the Normans, making Montevetuso a Norman-ruled city. Today, Norman architecture influences are evident throughout the city, seen in parts of the surrounding wall, the palazzo with a crenellated parapet, and the mullioned windows of the Benedictine Abbey. By the 1100s, the Benedictine Abbey had acquired the classification of ancient. The Normans introduced a feudal system in the region but did not change its name, Basilicata, which originated from the Greek word, *Basilikos,* representing the official sent from Constantinople to administer the territory during its Byzantine Empire period.

In subsequent decades, the region fell under the rule of other colonizers, primarily Spanish and French, including the Bourbon Dynasty. The last colonizing force was the House of Savoy, a dynasty that acquired territory in the western Alps, the kingdom of Sicily, and Sardinia.

Remarkably, to this day, the city, with its staggering history marked by a succession of invasions, reading like a tome of European history, remains steadfast, on that mountaintop, never sinking down beneath the ground, to land on the fallen ancient civilizations lying comatose in Dantesque layers, dreaming of great triumphs, which, in their DNA, bore the genes of decline.

Perched high on that mountain, there stood an alluring light rose-colored house, known as the house on Piazza Roma. It boasted the barrel-vaulted rooms characteristic of the adjacent tuff houses in Montevetuso. In a large, whitewashed bedroom with a vaulted ceiling of some fifteen feet and a red tiled floor, one day in August 1931, under the reign of the House of Savoy, I, Annalisa, was born. In the household, Mama, her siblings, and my grandparents, were in festive spirits as they cooed over the baby, who now became the center of their family life. However, beneath the jubilant façade, a profound and unspoken sadness lingered.

Beyond the confines of the house, life in Montevetuso proceeded through the daily routines. During the summer, much like that memorable day in August, a day might start at five or earlier in the morning. Peasants, with their brightly painted carts drawn by donkeys, roll downhill to the campagna, the cultivated area. This journey, which took some fifteen minutes by car, stretched to nearly an hour by donkey cart. The return journey in the late summer evening could be even lengthier. The city's streets, perched atop the mountain, generally ran uphill and downhill, leading residents to employ the verbs *ascendere* and *discendere,* when they set off from their houses to go up or down to another site in the city. In the event that the creaking wooden wagon wheels failed to rouse the city in the morning, the outlandish braying of the donkeys ricocheting from the stone contiguous houses and the cobblestone street constituted a remorseless reveille.

After the peasants passed through the streets, Nunzia, known as the goat woman, would occasionally appear, accompanied by her goat. She would stop at houses to inquire whether the signora would like some milk. A signora would emerge with a good-sized pot, and Nunzia would milk her goat on the spot. "Buon giorno," she would express with gratitude as she accepted her mere lira or two. "Buon giorno," the signora would respond, after which Nunzia would continue her solicitous walk along the cobblestone streets, she and her goat.

Shortly thereafter, Rosalia, the woman hired to transport the families' toilet crocks—the families who could afford to pay a lira or two--to the dumping site, made her rounds. And there appeared Nicola, delivering bread. Many kitchens then did not have ovens, and women brought their formed loaves of bread dough to the local furnace to be baked. There, they met other women and chatted as they waited for their bread to bake. Other women had their bread delivered. The baker's daughter, Nicola, along with others, would deliver the baked loaves. With her right hand, Nicola would balance five or six large loaves on a long board placed on her head. Sometimes, she would balance the long board on her left shoulder, keeping her right hand akimbo. She agilely managed Montevetuso's hilly streets, including that long staircase connecting a lower mountain level to a higher one. Around this time in the morning, Bèppe, the lamplighter, concluded his round of extinguishing the streetlamps. It was best to keep up friendly relations with Bèppe, or one might find one's street in darkness.

Meanwhile, in the rose-colored house on Piazza Roma, there was still much cooing over baby Annalisa accompanied by much crocheting of lace borders on the little baby gowns and bonnets and coverlets. However, shortly after her birth, Mama fell ill and could no longer supply the baby with milk. The family decided to buy goat's milk from Nunzia for the baby, but local peasant women insisted that donkey's milk was the best milk for the baby, though it was more expensive. Mama's family was better off than many other families in Montevetuso. Mama's sister, Raffaella, a schoolteacher, ten years older than Mama, and my grandfather, a carpenter who had emigrated to America twice, each time sending back a generous stipend, ensured that I was nourished with donkey's milk (which decades later, I learned was superior to both goat's and cow's milk).

As the months passed, despite the joy that baby Annalisa brought into the household, the delight in watching her grow and one day, smile, the unspoken sadness deepened and cast a shadow over the family, particularly Mama and my grandmother. Then the fateful day finally arrived.

In March, seven months after my August birth, my grandparents, Mama, and her siblings gathered before the grand double front doors of our house, all in tears. The women were wrapped in shawls, for even though spring arrives early in Southern Italy and in the almond trees in the campagna, the first to burst into glorious white blooms, awakening from winter dormancy, the morning air held a chilly edge. Standing before them was a well-dressed woman cradling a baby: Mama, holding me. In that unforgettable moment of that parting that marked the beginning of our journey to America, Mama, Annina, twenty-two years old, and equally tearful, repeatedly assured, "Yes, yes, of course, we will return for long visits," and her mother, my grandmother, also in tears, kept nodding and nodding, scarcely able to speak, knowing she would never see her daughter and granddaughter again.

As my grandmother held me for the last time in her arms, she lingered in that poignant moment before reluctantly handing me over to Mama. Among the tearful family standing at the double doors was one of her two sisters, Raffaella, the schoolteacher. She was my godmother. She was attractive, though not as beautiful as Mama, and there was something else noteworthy about her. She stood notably shorter than the rest of the family. What is her story? Raffaella, an unforgettable and heroic figure, will find her way through these pages.

It was now time to depart, as the bus driver, a fellow townsman, who had briefly stepped out of the small bus to commiserate during the emotional parting, reboarded the bus. Mama's trunk loaded, she, with me, and her father, my grandfather, who would accompany us to the port of Naples, stepped up into the bus to travel the twenty-six-minute journey to the train station in Naples, which took close to three hours.

In that way, on that fateful day in March, Mama and I bid farewell to our native home and country.

2

Journey to the New World

BY 1924, perhaps due to the endless influx to America of the "weary," the "poor," the "huddled masses," the "wretched refuse," and the "homeless, tempest-tost" (as Emma Lazarus eloquently put it), Congress placed a quota on immigrants from Eastern and Southern Europe, which included Italians, especially Southern Italians, like us. Mama and I, however, were not included in the quota. Mama's Italian passport bore the stamp *Fuori Quota*, signifying her status as the wife of a husband who had been in America for some ten years and was naturalized in 1928. I, on another hand, traveled as an American citizen, naturalized automatically through his citizenship. My red American passport, describing me as having light brown hair, blue eyes, and standing at two feet tall, was stated as being valid for two years. However, it was supplemented with an additional clause stipulating that the passport was valid for only two months and "solely for the journey to the United States." Mama's Italian passport was stamped with the seal of King Victor Emmanuel III of the House of Savoy.

As fate would have it, Mama and Papa were the only siblings

in their family who emigrated to America. Consequently, my sister Natalia and I grew up without the presence of grandparents, aunts, uncles, and first cousins, though there were sparse relatives of some remove. The quota indicated, of course, preferences of immigrants entering America, one of the considerations being the area of the globe the immigrants inhabited. From a practical standpoint, by that time, the New York City subway system had already been built, and the demand for Italian laborers had diminished, which possibly contributed to the introduction of the quota.

In those days, unlike today's somewhat impersonal airline travel, emigration to foreign countries marked moments of high, oh, yes, high drama. Imagine it!

A father, daughter, and granddaughter, stand at the Port of Naples, gazing upon the majestic transatlantic liner, the Augustus, moored at the Port. There is that final embrace between father, daughter, and granddaughter, and now Mama walks up the gangplank, baby in arms. She gazes back, almost ready to return, but her father signals her to continue. He had made the voyage to America twice, each time for a good several years, and worked in a piano factory. Those years had been among the most exhilarating years in his life. Twenty-two years later, during our return to Montevetuso, Mama would again embrace her father, now aged, and perhaps felt the presence of her mother nearby.

People on shore are waving white handkerchiefs, many with tears in their eyes, and some on board too, shed tears. Mama, with baby in arms, made her way to the stern and stood there, scanning the crowd for her father. There he was, waving a white handkerchief. Then—oh, the drama of that moment! —the transatlantic liner sounds three long foghorn blasts, reverberating far and wide over the Bay of Naples and striking clear into her heart, like a knell, a tolling of endings. Even as she gazed at the shore, the shores of Italy began to recede, and still recede, and the waving handkerchiefs look like faint white birds in the air. Oh, Italy!

Italy! cried Mama, inwardly. Oh, yes, yes, I will return soon, soon! Little did she know that in six years, 1938, war would erupt in Europe, followed by America's entry in 1941. The ocean she was about to cross would be patrolled by German submarines. Alas, that "soon, soon," would be elusive.

Now, on the ship, Italy and all other lands have vanished from sight, and all Mama sees for days on end are the unceasing undulations of waters sweeping over waters, the imperial domain of the Atlantic. Now, she realizes that she is alone, utterly alone! She knows nothing about this country, called *l'America*. And what did she know about this man, her husband. Certainly, their families knew each other, but her husband, that man, had been in America for a decade with only brief returns to Montevetuso.

Despite the Atlantic's occasional surging waves, Mama and I voyaged in comfort. Papa, who had honed his tailoring skills in Italy and become a skilled tailor, was working in a prestigious tailor shop on Fifth Avenue, in New York City. He could afford to summon us as Second Cabin Passengers, knowing that Steerage was shipped onto Ellis Island. The crew, cooing over the baby, the only one in Second Cabin Passengers, helped Mama with diapers, heating milk, and whatever other services were required. There were only thirty second-cabin passengers on that voyage, with twelve American citizens, which included me, and eighteen "aliens."

Finally, after approximately two weeks at sea, the passengers gathered at the bow, and with a feeling of great elation as they caught sight of her—Yes! It was truly she, the sole figure or fact that some, like Mama, knew about *l'America*. She stood there, crowned, and holding up her torch to illuminate the way—for them! Our transatlantic liner, the *Augustus*, reached its destination and docked at one of the ports of New York City.

Mama scanned the awaiting crowd. And then she saw him! There was Papa, eagerly awaiting us, the baby no longer swaddled but instead adorned in a new yellow printed cotton dress beneath her heavy wool bunting to meet Papa for the first time.

A year after his marriage in 1930, Papa left Montevetuso to return to work and resume life in America. He had wished to return to America with Mama, now pregnant, but my grandmother insisted that the baby be born in Italy. The decision was intended to ensure a smooth pregnancy for Mama amidst her family and to find comfort in the family's choice of a midwife. Reflecting back at that moment in my life, I suspect that beneath her concern for her daughter in her first pregnancy, my grandmother yearned to see the baby and be close to the baby, for a forbidding intuition within her darkly intimated that she would never again see the baby, this new member of the family.

Papa had not seen his wife for more than a year and, of course, the baby. The greetings and embraces at the New York City pier were matched with wonder, the wonder that circumstances had fallen into place, as if circumstances had miraculously aligned and infused routine life with an exceptional, unforgettable moment.

The taxicab awaited them. *"Andiamo a casa!"* said Papa, Home? thought Mama. Until now, *casa* had been that rose-colored house on the mountain. The taxicab drove on and on, streaming past new sights. This land was flat, flat, marveled Mama, looking out of the cab's window. She was no longer on a mountain with that vast, isolated, surround of a three-hundred-and sixty-five-degree panorama. The taxi streamed past buildings upon buildings and people everywhere and finally reaching the Bronx, stopped on Forest Avenue, an attractive residential block. Stepping out of the taxi, Mama, already overwhelmed with ever-new sights, took a quick look at the block where she would be living. She noticed red houses (which she later learned were brick houses), with spaces between them.

Something else was notable. Not a single goat or donkey could be seen on the street.

Now, Papa, holding me, in sheer delight, guided her upstairs to the second floor and their prepared, attractive apartment. *La casa.*

L'America, America.

3

Mama in America

IN THAT FIRST YEAR, living on Forest Avenue, in spring and summer, Mama still imagined she would be awakened in early morning by large cart wheels rolling along the cobblestone street and the jarring hee-hawing of donkeys. However, America greeted her with a different morning soundscape, a quiet one, though it had its unique sounds and animals. In some locations, milk and ice for the icebox were still delivered by horse and cart. Now, a horse replaced the donkey in Mama's everyday life, and milk was supplied by cows, not goats. One sound, the clinking of glass bottles as the milkman delivered the milk to porches, might have roused her, as it did the singer of Ella Mae Morse's popular 1943-44 war song, "Milkman, Keep Those Bottles Quiet."

Two years after her arrival in America, Mama gave birth to my sister, Natalia, an auspicious birthday in the Christmas-winter-solstice season, a time synonymous with lights and illuminations.

It was likely that had Mama not emigrated from Montevetuso, she might have lived in the mountaintop city all her life, but in America, her life led her from the Bronx to upstate New York, and finally to New England, to live close to me, where Natalia and I had decided to relocate her, judging it best, according to future circumstances.

Perhaps the most difficult change in Mama's life was the realization, eventually, that she had become dichotomous — half old world and half new world. She would never again perceive herself as one whole person. When she was in America, her neighbors saw her primarily as Italian; when she was in Italy, her relatives now viewed her as a good part American.

Being dichotomous meant that sometimes Mama thought in her native language, Italian, and sometimes in English. She spoke with a fairly strong Italian accent, though she had attended night school in the Bronx and gained adequate proficiency to become an American citizen during World War II. She had learned to read and to write in English, retaining the classic, even, straight script of the Italian forward-slanting hand, with characteristic volutes on capital letters, and she continued to cross her sevens, though early in her immigration, a cross bank teller said, "Don't cross your sevens!" Curiously, as a child, I was always surprised that my girlfriends' mothers spoke regular English. Mothers, I thought, had foreign accents. Having preceded Mama to America by twelve years, Papa wrote English quite well and had cultivated an attractive accent, a mixture of English and American pronunciations, but like many foreigners, he could not pronounce the fricative English *th* sound and would often omit the *h*.

Since Mama had emigrated with no knowledge of the English language, she had to diligently learn it here and did achieve an adequate knowledge to understand and carry on conversations. In Italy, she had continued her education beyond the level of other children at that time, even studying French, and she was more than proficient in her native language. In America, being constrained to express herself with a limited knowledge of English, she projected an inaccurate image of her abilities of articulation.

On one occasion, a friend of hers said to me, "Sometimes, I don't understand her."

Probably, Mama had not perceived the diminished image she would convey in America, as an immigrant woman with a pronounced accent. As the years passed by, and she became aware of her limitations in expressing her ideas, was she disturbed? disheartened? Possibly, but Mama, along with other countless women immigrants, particularly her contemporaries, heroically gave all her efforts to building a solid life amid family and friends in the country of the "golden door," however foreign some customs were to her and however heartsick she might have felt, recalling the warm, familiar customs of Italy.

Mama emigrated knowing little or nothing of the New World and was dependent on Papa. However, her resolute nature slowly pushed her towards independence. Possessing basic sewing skills, she managed to get a job in a nearby sewing shop, coordinating with our school hours. Now she was making her own little salary. But she did not tell Papa she was working. The comical twist to this story was that Mama and Papa were invited to a friend's small party, and there, also invited, was the owner of the local sewing shop! Recognition and laughter brought all to a happy ending, and Mama continued working.

Throughout the passing decades of her life in America, it was part of Mama's sanguine temperament to be open and enterprising, to fall into the customary ways of spending the hours of the everyday in the New World. No, dinner was not partaken midday in the New World; no, the midday siesta was not in character with the capitalistic verve of the New World. Mama was to live into the twenty-first century, always maintaining that openness to making the most of the changing circumstances of her life as she aged.

Reflecting how Mama spent the last years of her life, I was made keenly aware that after all, the underpinnings of daily life were the unsung, unsalaried routines marking the hours of a day, the rituals of mealtimes, making lunch and dinner, possibly, an afternoon rest or nap or a television program. Maybe for her, the best antidote to the poignancy of growing old and becoming dependent on others was that morning aroma of percolating coffee, defining each new day, each successive day, yes, toward one hundred years old and beyond. There was much to be grateful for in waking up to another day of mortality. These small and yet tenacious routines that define our daily life afford it a semblance of sanity in a world that may be meaningless without our construct of it.

To break the long solitary afternoons in this ever-foreign country, Mama established the ritual of making espresso coffee at four o'clock. The aroma itself, filling the three rooms, uplifted her spirits. Sitting alone, in her nicely furnished and comfortable apartment, she gave herself up to memory and nostalgia, as she sipped the flavor of that long ago home, three thousand miles or so away. In the early years of her emigration, she made Italian coffee in the Neapolitan drip pot (the Neapolitans are said to make the best coffee). The Moka espresso pot gained popularity decades later. Mama eventually learned to make American percolated coffee, which she termed, "brown coffee" to distinguish it from espresso, which she referred to as "black coffee."

In her delicate floral porcelain demitasse, measuring a mere four ounces or less, were immeasurable quantities of memories: evocative sensations—aromas, vivid images of family and friends, laughing, crying, waving— sensations that would remain with her, forever, the length of the rest of her life and maybe even permanently somewhere in the ether, keeping within its molecular structures the annals of the earth. Every so often, a singular image emerges before her: she, in her maroon Inverness coat and small-rimmed beige hat in *stile aeronatico*, her baby Annalisa, in her arms, and her mother standing before her, both in tears. The day of emigration, the moment of farewell, she, twenty-two years old, assuring her mother, of course she would return. But she, the mother, intuiting the future, knew. She knew deep down this was their last meeting, the last time their voices would cross that forbidding ocean. But no, Mama did not want to take the last sip of espresso with that poignant memory of mother and daughter. Instead, she summoned up the memory of her beautiful younger self, newly emigrated, eager to embrace the New World.

She often reminisced about those grand moments when Papa took her on the subway from the Bronx to Manhattan, to see the new Empire State Building, finished in 1931, just before our arrival in 1932; to the old Metropolitan Opera House, with its famous gold curtain and "Diamond Horseshoe" shape; to Radio City Hall, which opened in 1932, and at Christmas, to marvel at the lighted tree at Rockefeller Center and gala store decorations. Italian emigrants sailing to the New World never forgot the wonders of Christmas lights and store window decors they beheld in New York City. Their amazement was akin to Dorothy's when she first glimpsed the Emerald City in the Land of Oz.

Aside from the awe Mama felt at beholding the celebrated sites of Manhattan, the greatest moments of fascination descended upon her in far less spectacular places, like her visits to the local fabric store, its wall lined with bolts of solid and variegated colors, of untold varieties of designs. She would finger the fabrics: batiste, muslin, percale, chiffon, dotted swiss, organdy, piqué, silk and satin, densely piled velvet, corduroy; her choices to be sewn on our treadle 1920s Singer sewing machine, used primarily by Papa for his tailoring work. He never converted to what Mama colorfully referred to as a "power machine," meaning an electric sewing machine. Eventually she learned to use one, working in a small factory, becoming an expert on the exacting skill of turning collars and cuffs of men's shirts.

Our family never bought ready-made clothes. Mama crafted

our dresses and skirts and blouses, and Papa, our suits and coats. Natalia and I in our neatly ironed or sometimes starched look, moved a bit formally in our organdy dresses, falling crisply from waist downward; I delighted in the swishing sound of taffeta with my every step. Showing off before my girlfriends, I twirled round and round in my woolen red plaid amply flared skirt; and I felt like a young movie star—an Elizabeth Taylor, of those days--in a green, velvet dress, with a white satin collar and white satin small bows down the bodice. Corduroy? That was the boys' sound, their velvety ribbed corduroy pants, squishing, as they walked up and down the classroom aisles. Eventually, toward midcentury, girls occasionally wore what were called, "slacks," casual pants, actually an adoption of a man's trousers that were not part of a suit. A decade or two later, jeans became a national and global wardrobe staple.

We often wore the popular jumpers, though of Mama's unique design: a skirt with a bodice comprised of two panels sweeping over the shoulders. As was fashionable then, Mama occasionally made "mother and daughter" dresses. One memorable set featured the three of us in a brown taffeta skirt and a beige bow tie blouse. Influenced by the widely popularized Good Neighbor Policy toward Latin America, Mama made us boleros, a short sleeveless jacket open in front, possibly related to the slow Spanish dance, Bolero, made famous by Ravel. President Roosevelt's 1930s Good Neighbor policy was also amply reflected in popular culture and songs, which crooners sang over the airwaves. Even now, I can hear some of the songs: "South of the Border, down Mexico Way," "Bésame Mucho," "How I Love the Kisses of Dolores, Not Marie or Emily or Doris. In Hollywood musicals, we gazed wide-eyed at the dashing "Rumba King," Xavier Cugat, and the inimitable Carmen Miranda dancing the samba, with the latter sporting a hat adorned with fruit. The two timeless songs emerging from the Good Neighbor cultural movement were "Cielito Lindo," and "La Paloma."

As the years passed for Mama in America, her English steadily improved, yet she still retained a discernable, though somehow attractive foreign accent. Despite adapting to the New World, she felt mostly at ease amongst Italians. However, she was always that plucky young woman who bravely left her family to emigrate to America. With that same pluckiness she fell into the usages of the New World. Boleros? Yes, she would make boleros. On one Halloween, she purchased bundles of crepe paper, sat at the Singer sewing machine and transformed Natalia and me into two young gypsy girls with ruffled crepe paper dresses. Yet, she had never heard of the celebration of Halloween, for it did not exist in Italy until it was exported there in the global twenty-first century.

4

Customs and Cuisine

In America, Mama, now embracing her Italian American identity, blended the domestic customs of Italy with new domestic traditions of America. Her culinary expertise remained deeply rooted in Italian cuisine. She was adept at making perfect frittatas, favoring asparagus frittatas. Her traditional lentil soup, influenced by the flavors of southern Italian cuisine, featured ingredients such as a can of tomato sauce, garlic, olive oil, celery, carrots, and sparse linguine pasta, broken into one inch or so pieces. Mama's preferred vegetable was boiled escarole, vibrant green but tender, seasoned with salt to taste, olive oil, and garlic.

Our meals were consistently prepared with fresh ingredients. In our community then, supermarkets were nonexistent. We relied on local fruit and vegetable markets or purchased from truck vendors. The colorful fruit added to our perceptions of the changing seasons. Winter brought us the cheerful presence of oranges, and oranges brightly colored our Christmas dinner table, served cut in thin rounds opened like a fan and perched over the stemmed wine glasses. In the summertime, we eagerly awaited the highly reputed Georgia peaches, which we sometimes sliced and soaked in our stemmed wine glasses. Indispensable at Christmastime were chestnuts, roasted and piping hot from the kitchen oven. The aroma alone evoked memories of the great city of New York and Fifth Avenue with its spectacular storefront windows, the towering Rockefeller Center brilliantly lit Christmas tree, and there, perhaps on a corner was the chestnut man, roasting chestnuts. In my youth, the vendors were typically Italian, likely immigrants themselves, offering a product familiar to their origins, for chestnuts were imported from Central Italy. The smell of the chestnuts I would buy transported me back to the warm, comforting aroma of chestnuts at my childhood Christmas dinners in the Bronx.

The emergence of airplanes (referred to as air freighters at the time) revolutionized our concept of seasonal food consumption. We marveled as we learned that now fresh fruit and berries from the Pacific Northwest could be brought to eastern markets in a sixteen-hour overnight trip. Even more astonishing, we discovered that post World War II, no location on the globe would be more than sixty-hours away from us by air travel. (Jet planes were yet in the far future.)

Mama's midday Sunday dinner became a cherished tradition, one I carried with me into my own household in later years. Her unwavering menu featured pasta and meatballs, and occasionally, braciole. Mama often prepared a generous serving which I would bring to our elderly neighbors next door, Mr. and Mrs. Strausner. They resided in a very modest blue shingled house, which was eventually torn down after they died. Mama took great pride in her classic tomato sauce and meatballs. In her nineties, she was afflicted with macular degeneration, but with her strong, undaunted spirit, she continued to cook her Sunday tomato sauce and other accustomed dishes, relying more on touch and intuition than vision.

Our dinners, including our simple daily ones, were typically served in courses, following the Italian tradition. The *primo piatto* (first course) was usually the vegetable or vegetable combined with pasta, a favorite combination being pasta e piselli. Alternatively, the *primo piatto* could consist of soup or pasta with a tomato sauce. The *secondo piatto* was a choice of meat, fish, or perhaps some other source of protein.

When we had guests, Mama's meals achieved a virtuosic series of courses. Added to the meatballs in the tomato sauce were the braciole and sausages. Roast chicken followed with a side dish of asparagus or artichokes, parboiled, dipped in flour and eggs, and sautéed in olive oil. An occasional side dish was sautéed lamb's brains, also parboiled and dipped in flour and eggs before meeting the skillet.

On occasion, following the preparation of those grand meals for company, Mama developed a ferocious headache and nausea. For relief, she would slice a raw potato and secure the slices against her forehead using a large white handkerchief. Then she would lie in bed, potato treated. I assumed that she took recourse in some old wives' remedy she learned in Italy, and in my imagination, I pictured these women, all in forever-black mourning, except for the flash of a seventeen-gold carat earring, worn day and night. Decades later, I would come to understand the medicinal value of the humble potato. It's possible that, used as Mama did, the cut slices released juices that helped alleviate the intensity of the headache.

Mama's cuisine included garlic, basil, arugula, broccoli rabe, linguine with clam sauce, panettone, and pesto (the latter two introduced after World War II), along with olive oil as a staple. These were foods she never dreamed would emerge into popular American usage. "Garlic eaters" was a pejorative term sometimes used to describe Italians. We first encountered pesto when we visited my aunt in Genoa, in 1955, for pesto is uniquely Genoese. A perfect rendering of pesto requires, as my aunt professed, the small-leaved basil, grown under the aegis of the breezes from the Ligurian Sea with its salty air and Genoa's measure of sunshine. Pesto was unknown in the United States until decades after the 1950s.

Having introduced the term, "Garlic eaters," I will also mention that during the thirties and forties, foreign customs and perhaps dress, were met with reservation or negative reactions. Since I was born in Italy, my ears were pierced in infancy, though Mama was miffed with the woman piercing me, for she pierced the right ear asymmetrically higher than the left. However, upon immigrating to the United States, I never made use of the pierced ears. In those days, all were to be melted in the melting pot of America. My friends in immigrant households and Natalia and I, in mine, were not encouraged to speak the foreign language our parents spoke, though we understood it. As we grew into adults, we discovered that stepping into the melting pot, especially for Southern Europeans like Southern Italians, the ingredients did not homogenize but remained quite lumpy. We realized that it would take more than one generation to meld the ingredients into a smooth porridge. The essence of America's melting pot was a dynamic process of moving from lumpiness to a smooth blend.

Clearly, in those days, seeing me entering kindergarten wearing earrings would have marked me as a foreigner, a greenhorn, with perhaps not altogether congenial ethnic connotations. The first earrings I wore as a young woman were for nonpierced ears. I started to use earrings for pierced ears at twenty-one years old! Whatever the Italian woman did, however asymmetrical, the pierced points in my ears, unused for about two decades, remained open and available.

Foreign names were also met with reservation by American

society, perhaps names like Nina, Annalisa, Concetta, Natalia, Helina (my Polish friend's name). The name *Rocco*, revered in Montevetuso as its patron saint, might well be changed to Robert by Italian men for a better chance to get a job, particularly during World War II. At Ellis Island, immigration personnel occasionally changed the surnames of immigrants to more familiar American ones, and these families went through life with a different identity than their actual nationality. American society also looked askance at ethnic foods, such as lamb's brains, the Italian *soffritto*, which in our kitchen included offal, certain fish such as eel or carp and other seemingly bizarre foods such as escargot and frog's legs, the French delicacy.

For many years after our arrival in America, as perhaps was the case for other families at that time, we did not have a telephone. However, we managed our lives very well without one. When we finally did install one in our house, Mama rarely used it, feeling diffident about talking into this strange black apparatus, especially with her Italian accent. Mama's elderly Italian friend, Giovanna, picked up a ringing phone for the first time, and upon hearing a voice, thought she heard squawks and gurgles, and told Mama there was a parrot at the other end.

As was common during that time, we never owned an automobile. The only pedals my father was interested in were the pedals on a piano. Accommodating customers without telephones and automobiles, neighborhood merchants would come to the house, take orders, and then return with the merchandise. Truck venders, parking on the rural Bronx streets, would loudly and scarcely comprehensibly call out their apples and fresh spinach or their flounders and fillet sole. Women would emerge from their homes in the standard wraparound printed cotton house dress. Some truck venders continued their neighborhood circuits all year round.

Not long after we emigrated from Italy, Mama, feeling nostalgic for her Italian Christmases, tried something new. Typically, on Christmas Eve, in Southern Italy, fish cooked in various ways was the traditional dinner. Among the served fish were baccalà and baked eel (the female eel, the *capitone,* as it was meatier than the male). One year, the day before Christmas Eve, Mama bought a live *capitone* from a fish vender, who explained that to kill it, she had to simply let the water out and throw salt on it.

With some hesitation, she carried the bag containing the squiggly eel upstairs to the second floor, entered the kitchen, and filled the washtub with a good amount of cold water. Then she dumped the eel into its new habitat. The eel seemed to happily swim around the tub, thinking, perhaps, that it was in the Mediterranean Sea, but I, quite young though old enough to know that there was a creature in the tub that looked like a snake, was not as happy as the eel, nor, I think, was Mama. She quickly covered the tub with the board serving as a countertop but left several inches open for ventilation.

When Papa came home, he was happy to learn that he would once again enjoy the traditional *capitone* as an added fish to the Christmas Eve dinner.

"But you have to kill the eel!" declared Mama, and explained to Papa how easy it was to carry out the execution of the eel. "Me!" Papa's happiness quickly turned to horror. He walked over to the washtub, lifted the lid, looked at the happily swimming eel, shuddered, and quickly closed the lid. "If it is so easy to kill it, you kill it," he said to Mama, turned away, and disappeared into the parlor.

The next day, on Christmas Eve, the eel was still swimming in the makeshift Mediterranean Sea. However, Christmas Eve dinner was traditionally served late, after which some families would then prepare to attend Midnight Mass. There was still time to execute the eel (though by now, Mama began to have a nightmare feeling that she would have to live with this eel for days on end). Fortunately, she had invited two cousins, couples, for dinner, which promised a possible recourse.

Here they were, and she cheerfully announced that tonight's dinner would include a specialty, a *capitone*, though she had to explain one crucial point for all to enjoy it. The eel must be killed! But killing it was easy.

"Luigi," Mama said, beginning to panic, "Please, would you—"

"Me!" cried Luigi, aghast, and he drew back against the kitchen wall, hands over his breast. Luigi, a kind, mild man, passionate about his flower garden, killed only Japanese beetles invading his roses.

Now in a panic, Mama turned to Agostino. "Agostino, please!"

"Me!" cried Agostino, his eyes nearly popping out of his head, his face contorted with horror. Agostino, also a kind, mild man, was a trolley car mechanic who rather than killing, brought dead trolley cars back to life.

Now, desperate and hopelessly wishing that the eel were back in the sea and not in her washtub, Mama took recourse to her next door neighbor, a hunter whose wife was accustomed to seeing creatures in various bloody states, and through her, the wife, with knife, hatchet, whatever other tools (everyone had fled to the parlor), the now murdered eviscerate, and peeled eel met its inglorious end. By then, Mama was thoroughly sickened by the eel, which was no longer a gourmet food but a haunting reminder of her ordeal over it and of the eel's own personal ordeal. She hastily put the eel into the oven to bake.

Mama's Christmas Eve dinner that year, fueled by heavy nostalgia, featured its usual spectacular table of fish—baccalà prepared in a tomato sauce and served with linguine (or spaghetti), and *in bianco* (in white), that is, poached and served with salt, black pepper, and olive oil; squid (calamari), fish fillets breaded and sautéed, and the celebrated or uncelebrated eel. Everyone indulged heartily in every delectable fish, except the eel, which untouched, went into the garbage. And the diners philosophically concluded that if one consumed the creatures of the earth, it was better not to know anything about their transit from life to death.

What the fish vender did not tell Mama was that sprinkling the eel with salt (a measured amount) didn't immediately result in the merciful death of the eel. After the eel finally succumbed to the salt, naturally, mama would have to wipe off the slime and peel the skin to prepare the eel for her to bake. Fortunately, the gruesome task was taken on by the neighbor's wife, who entered the scene like a deus ex machina. In any case, whether hammered or knifed to death, that Christmas Eve eel never died.

The celebration and perception of Christmas in America was itself among the new customs that Mama found to be astonishingly different. What curious imagery portrayed the season! In Italy, the imagery of Christmas summoned up shepherds, herding sheep, and bagpipes, some still playing lively pieces, perhaps from pagan times, and for a house decoration, possibly, sprigs from an orange tree. Christmas was pastoral, represented in music in the pastorale.

In America, the imagery of Christmas summoned up the Christmas milieu of Northern Europe: Santa Claus, snow, reindeer, and the lighted Christmas tree. In the era of television, initiating globalization, the Northern European Christmas was imported by Montevetuso, and a brilliantly lit Christmas tree is erected on Piazza Roma evoking snowy landscapes and evergreens in an ancient land whose very essence is contained in groves of fig and olive trees. But Mama had emigrated in the days when the bagpipers marched along the cobblestone streets.

Mama transitioned easily from bagpipers and orange sprigs to sleighs and reindeer, but most of all to a lit Christmas tree, which, in some fairy-tale fashion, to her and perhaps others, summoned up a feel of cheer, of momentarily doing away with adult worries and heavy introspective ponderings, to find oneself in the aura of the sweet wonder of childhood. A Christmas tree with lights and silver icicles stood in our parlor every year even as, celebrating Christmas Eve, Papa sat at our foot-pumped harmonium, placed near the piano, and played a lively shepherd bagpipe song.

Years later, in her 80s, when Mama lived in her third-floor apartment near me, she put up a small artificial Christmas tree hung with blue lights and positioned it in front of the large window of her living room. Every year, in the evening, we took the elevator to the ground floor, walked outside, and looked up at her window to behold the blue-lit tree and the blue candles on adjacent large windows on either side. It was a simple ritual that added a touch of festivity to the holiday season.

It struck me how little it took to infuse life with sweetness. The color *blue* summoned up in me another object which sweetened my childhood remembrances. When I was nine or ten, Mama gave me a blue plastic bracelet, about one inch wide, slipped on and off accordion style, a simple bagatelle, probably bought at the then popular Woolworth's Department Store. I was enchanted. Wearing the bracelet, I was Dorothy wearing her magic ruby red shoes, in *The Wizard of Oz*, which I saw contemporaneously at the local Bronx Loews movie theater. Throughout my life, I received some lovely gifts, including cultured pearls, gemstone necklaces, but the pleasure I took in such necklaces never equaled the delight and special privilege I felt wearing the blue plastic bracelet.

Where is that bracelet now, aside from being immortalized in one of the many closets of the brain, the closets the brain reserves for memories. Where is Mama's artificial Christmas tree today?

What happens to things, for they constitute the fabric of our everyday lives. An old water fountain pen, a favorite skirt, a bow tie blouse, a shoulder strap bag of soft Italian leather, daily slippers even worn out of shape, a favorite tool--a spirit planar with its magical leveling liquid--an old bathrobe starting to shred, perhaps cozier psychologically than physically, even a creaky floorboard in a bedroom, which becomes a friendly assurance of normality in a day's routine. Perhaps some are finally incinerated and become ashes, like us. Ashes to ashes.

Customs, like physical objects, give structure to our everyday and help our consciousness construe the nature of our reality, the reality of our little life. When saying good-bye, whether when I was at Mama's apartment or she at my house, she and I would follow our good-byes with waving, from windows or outside our doors, as seasons permitted.

In those years when Mama lived in that third-floor apartment, the visits were more than just casual encounters. She would make lunch for me, sometimes a delicious frittata or her hearty lentil soup. Then we would go to a café for coffee and a sweet, often a muffin, after which we shopped together for groceries. After helping her bring the groceries to her apartment, I would leave. As my car passed by her front windows, I would slow down and see her up there waving good-bye to me, and I would wave good-bye. In November and December, when I would leave between four thirty and five, it was dark, and I would see her up at the window, waving good-bye to the headlights of the car. After she died, and I happened to be in the vicinity of the apartment, I would look up and see her there, waving good-bye.

Another custom deeply etched in my mind was to dial the *three-rings signal*. In those far-off early telephone days, charges for long-distance phoning were prohibitive. In our household, not only did we delay installing a phone, but we also used it frugally and only for local calls. We established a code for calls out of the local area, which I used as an adult living elsewhere. I would ring my family home three times and immediately hang up to indicate my safe arrival, knowing mama anxiously awaited those three rings.

I can hear her now, "Three rings, three rings."

5

Mama's Last Years

When Mama was in her nineties, we embarked on a poignant journey to select burial plots in a cemetery. The decision was made with great thought and consideration. The cemetery site was composed of soothing rolling hills. An impressive granite structure in a gothic style, with a large pointed central arch, flanked on each side with lower chapel-like extensions announced the entrance to this silent undulant city of the dead, its tombstones and sculptures eloquent with the funerary language of marble and granite. Here and there, an angel with outspread wings rose up from a knoll, like a resurrection; here and there, a soaring obelisk rose up from another knoll, slender and funereally Egyptian, evoking testaments to the dead.

Together, mama and I walked along the silent, peaceful paths of the cemetery to examine sites available and for mama to choose one that would meet with her approval. It was a warm summer day and Mama was wearing her black dress printed with small roses. Despite her age, she still had good posture and walked easily along with me.

Papa, who passed away at the age of fifty-six while we resided in the East Bronx, was buried in a cemetery in the Bronx, within view of the Bronx Whitestone Bridge, in a gravesite designated for two occupants. He remained very much alive in our memory, particularly when we heard piano pieces he frequently played, such as the first movement of the *Moonlight Sonata,* emulating the celebrated performance of it by the then live and famous Ignacy Paderewski. Papa also liked to play pieces by Enrique Granados. However, his signature piece was "Papillon" (Butterfly), from Edvard Grieg's *Lyric Pieces.*

With the unpredictable twists of family life and with far-off new addresses that shaped our family's fate, Papa languished alone in the Bronx cemetery. Had we continued to live in New York City, Mama would have perceived that vacant compartment as her rightful place, but now we were constrained to choose a new burial site.

We walked solemnly, not to disturb the quiet entombed dust, for as Emily Dickinson wrote, "This quiet Dust was Gentlemen and Ladies / And Lads and Girls – / Was laughter and ability and sighing / And Frocks and Curls." Coming to one of the available sites on the road level, landscaped with a row of boxwood hedges, accessible even during the snow and ice of winter, I asked Mama what she thought.

"No," Mama said, shaking her head. "I don't like it here. It would be too damp!"

Dampness signified mold, decay, and to Mama, a historic dread of it, for dampness could lead to rheumatism, arthritis, unwonted pains and aches, and even strange diseases, like the fatal one that struck her beloved older sister Raffaella. In Montevetuso, the houses, all contiguous, were constructed of tufa. Stone, stone, stone, everywhere, all the rooms in our natal house, barrel-vaulted, were of stone, and in Mama's childhood, there was no central heating. She recalled how she and her siblings, wearing bulky handmade woolen underwear, huddled close to the brazier, almost scorching their legs, to ameliorate the coldness of winter and the dreaded dampness that hung about other parts of the unheated house. Oh, the perilous dampness. "No, not here." After all, in ancient times, weren't cities, including Montevetuso, built on mountainsides? Why? Not only as protection from marauders but also to escape malaria mosquitoes. Malaria was bad air (mal) (aria), dampness!

But thankfully, Italy's winter is short, and the dry golden heat of the Mediterranean sun vanquishes dampness. How comfortable then are the cool barrel-vaulted rooms, with the heavy wooden shutters shut against that African sun, or more modernly, the Venetian type blinds, the *persiane,* drawn down full length. Yet, be warned: if breezes flow through open doors in the house, resulting in cross-ventilation, that is, causing a draft, a dreaded *corrente,* even in ninety-degree-heat, shut the doors! Perhaps that was what happened to Mama's beloved sister Raffaella: she had been caught in a pernicious draft, though there was another possible cause. The sirocco, a warm, humid southeast wind, originating in the Sahara as a dry, dusty wind, gathers moisture as it traverses the Mediterranean Sea. When it sweeps over Southern Italy, beware! for it is held responsible for rheumatic diseases and other undiagnosable maladies.

As a child, Raffaella would play with her sister and her friends, swinging on a hoop nailed to the archway over the descending stone staircase to the lower level of contiguous houses on the cobblestone streets. Perhaps during one of those moments, the sirocco, crossing the Ionian Sea, scaled the mountain and swept over the city, its sinuous ghostly sweeping mists engulfing the cathedral, the campanile, the clock tower, and reaching the children, engulfed them before they had time to flee home. Perhaps, that is when the malady struck, for when she was eleven years old, Raffaella, fell sick. The sinister disease wormed itself through her graceful, budding body, gravely afflicting the spine, and within several years, the adult Raffaella emerged stunted and slightly humped. Drafts, humid winds, low grounds, all were culprits harboring dampness.

"No, not here," Mama had said; "it would be too damp." After all, there was no denying that exacerbated by dampness, as Mama believed, decay would swiftly take hold, followed by the emergence of maggots and worms, and then the unthinkable. Having dismissed the lower realms of the cemetery, Mama looked around the cemetery grounds and gazed up at the highest hill. "That is where I want to be buried!" Yes, high, as was the remote Southern Italian hill city in which she was born, there, at least immune from malaria and other toxic essences. Very well! The burial site was secured, and in time, as I had foreseen, in winter, usually snowbound, the road is closed off to vehicles, and I must trudge up the hill to reach the burial site and visit Mama, a feat that becomes more arduous for me as I age. Nonetheless, I was happy to think: no, no dampness for Mama up there, much closer to the sky, only sweet solacing breezes.

Mama had once been hailed as one of the most beautiful women in her Italian hometown, and Papa affectionately called her *La Gioconda*. In her last years, her face was marked by eyebags and many wrinkles. Even in her nineties, she diligently applied cold washcloths to the bags, hoping they would shrink. Looking in the mirror, at the disheartening specter of herself, she would say, "I do not want to go out anymore and have people see me." Well, I thought, hadn't Anna Magnani said that she earned every one of her wrinkles? Mama's wrinkles, in their own way, carried the weight of three thousand miles of ocean and of two continents, the one, native, no longer accessible, forever a heartache; the other, foreign, sometimes humiliating, often confusing, always challenging, finally adjusted to, but never completely assimilated.

Yet aging, wrinkles, that specter in the mirror, a changing

figure, requiring adjustments in clothes, would never deter Mama's strong spirit to keep up appearances as well as to participate in senior activities. She had always been meticulous about her appearance and clothes, washing by hand her Italian sweaters made from the finest wool and often decorated with an embroidered flower or two, keeping them in prime condition. As she aged, she would lament that she could no longer wear her stylish Italian shoes, especially those netted beige pumps, and was constrained to wear stodgy black Mary Jane shoes and occasionally sneakers. Later, confined to a wheelchair, she lamented that her wardrobe now consisted solely of pants, with her dresses and bold-printed tops becoming a relic of the past.

Yet, in aging Mama was to discover that she had to maintain that strong spirit not only to bear up to physical decline but also to withstand the views of the aged by society and the occasional dismaying remarks. At the age of ninety, she had a minor heart attack. As she lay in the hospital, the young intern (far from even the mere idea that one day he would confront death) said, "Well, you are ninety. You have had a good long life." Mama was silent. What use was there to reply to that? Whether you are thirty or ninety, you do not want to die. The distance between the yet green mind of youth and the seasoned mind of age is insurmountable. Mama lived on for more than another decade. Always courageous in spirit, she withstood the distressing remarks or observations she was to meet with in random circumstances. In her late nineties she retained a good number of her teeth. The first remark a doctor made as he prepared to examine her was, "Take out your teeth."

But a strong spirit, the commitment to maintaining appearances, and adhering to a healthy Mediterranean diet, did not obviate destiny's chance or predestined happenings to change the course of a life.

Mama had reached the age of ninety-eight and was still managing housekeeping chores and making me lunch every

Wednesday. One day, in her apartment, she tripped or perhaps bent over to pick up something, and she fell. Unable to get up and knowing she had seriously hurt her leg, she managed to drag herself to the phone and phone Natalia and me.

That marked the end of an era in our family and for us, Mama and me. Our Sunday dinners, Wednesday lunches and shopping together, coffee in cafés, attending local plays and operas became part of family history, of memories, and perhaps of reminiscent chapters in a book.

Inevitably, Mama entered a nursing home, which Natalia and I selectively chose, and which, importantly, was within several miles from me. Three years later, she passed away, three months short of her one hundred and second birthday.

6

Remembering Mama

As TIME WENT by and I no longer felt secure driving up that steep hill to visit Mama, I climbed up slowly on foot, resting at intervals. I liked to think of my visits as a pilgrimage. Walking through the cemetery from my parked car, I became familiar with its residents, or rather its representatives of its residents. I passed the green statue of the seated cloaked-draped figure, with beautifully sculptured androgynous facial features. The statue's head is thrust back and its eyes are half shut, forever frozen in a death swoon. Higher up, I passed the little girl leaning against the flowered rail, one hand supporting her chin, perhaps caught up in Alice-in-Wonderland dreams; and the standing young woman in a draped gown holding a bouquet of flowers, youth, that would never grow old, a bouquet that would never wilt. Another young woman in a draped gown, seated, one hand holding flowers, the other supporting her head, lies in everlasting pensiveness, perhaps caught up in youthful dreams of glowing futures only to learn that she is doomed. The dog, sitting atop a gravestone, looks forever for its master, and the recumbent naked male figure, with fig leaf, is youth eternal, immortalized in stone.

Eventually, I reached Mama's gravesite and stood before the handsome Salisbury pink granite gravestone, its headstone decorated with an incised arabesque design at each top corner. My eyes dropped to the large rectangular space given over to the inhabitant the pink stone sheltered, the name and dates of her life. I read and reread the solemn inscription. Of course, the name and dates, inscribed in stone, could not be undone. They were immutable; they bore the solid verity of stone. The dates were a stark fact, that stern, implacable word, admitting of no reversal.

Mama was gone. She had lived for one hundred years and not quite two years; she had lived from one century, the twentieth, to another, the twenty-first. Over the course of her remarkably long life, she went from hearing the news proclaimed by the town crier in her Italian birthplace to receiving the daily newspaper at her door in America. From travelling by horse and carriage to owning her own car. As life sped faster, distances seem to become shorter. Once having to wait three or four months for mail by sea, she experienced the astonishing circa two-week speed of air mail and finally, to her wonder, the marvel of near instantaneous email, though by then no longer within her compass of learning and putting into practice.

"Mama," I called out, in the silent city around me, "if you had lived to experience the magic of ZOOM, you would have actually seen, and talked to, all your Italian relatives in Italy, as if they were right there in the room with you!" Mama's mother died during World War I1, and aside from not seeing her mother ever again after her emigration, living three thousand miles across the Atlantic, she could hardly sit at her bedside those last hours.

But I could do that here, where Natalia and I relocated her. During those final days, I sat at the side of Mama's bed in the nursing home, feeling numb, unable to fully grasp this transition I was witnessing —the passing of a human being from be-ing to not being. This was the dire hour that she, one hundred and one years old, just three months short of her birthday, was dying, eating no more, rising no more, eyes closed, in a somnolence induced by gentle Morpheus, in small dosages of his essence, morphine. Mama was dying, dying, I iterated and reiterated, to grasp the import of that word, but though I held her hand, though I spoke softly, endearingly, though I gently passed my hand over her forehead in a slow, repeated motion, to gather myself close to her, the concept of dying, even of my mother, remained abstract. The glow of life, all those cells within me still busily functioning, created an impasse between us. Mama was drifting beyond my reach. Would the collection of precious particles that constituted the essence of Mama's personality, that *was* Mama, disintegrate upon the expiration of this decomposing body under the blanket? Would the immaterial substance remain intact in some form after the body, the material substance, the living cells closed down? I felt a huge existential anguish to think that it was indeed altogether possible that she, Mama, the person herself, was expiring here before me with the expiring body.

On one of those days, sitting quietly by her bedside as she lay in a moribund state, comforted by morphine, I put my ear close to her mouth, for she was whispering a brief word or two over and over, from which I could distinguish only *eses*. Then I understood: *la casa, la casa, la casa*—home. Was home in the Bronx, to which she emigrated? No. Was home in northern New England, to which she was relocated? No. Home was Italy, Montevetuso, her childhood home, surrounded by her beloved family, parents and siblings. The irony of emigrants, or at least, of Mama was that despite being haunted by her family and life in Montevetuso, she could not return there and live again as the Italian she once was. Nor was her family, parents dead and siblings married, the same as it once was.

In the last three years of her life, spent in the nursing home, occasionally, as the desire rose to the fore with insupportable intensity, she would grab an aide's arm and beg her to take her home; she, Mama, would pay her! I could only imagine Mama's anguish, the despairingly dreadful knowledge that she was helpless, she who was reaching her hand across the Atlantic, fancying a hand reaching out to her across the sea to America, and she could not even rise from her wheelchair to grasp the hand and make her way home. And there were those other passing occasions when Mama realized the hopeless, the helpless, unredeemable stage in life she had lived on to, those moments when lucidly she made a statement or so to the aides, and whether because of her accent or because she was now over one hundred years old, aides just smiled and paid little heed to her remark.

Were we, then, like Cassandra in our old age? Did no one heed our words anymore? Did others equate our physical helplessness and our worn, lined countenance with a parallel appearance of our mind, which in their perception would now be reduced in size and shriveled, a mere walnut shell responding incoherently or irrelevantly to the animated world about us?

Sometimes, Mama and I would sit across from each other in her pleasant room at the nursing home. She would be in her wheelchair, and I in a small blue upholstered sofa chair, both of us looking out the picture window at a large lawn on which we could see the windows of adjacent nursing home residents. We would observe the sudden flights of starlings or mourning doves perched on a telephone wire, delighting Mama. She saw them, though she had macular degeneration. Then she would look at me and ask, "How is Mama?" I replied, "She is well." She remained silent; however much her mind took refuge in the unreality of sweet past life within her family and however much she persisted in asking that question, on a deeper level, she knew that her mother was dead. Sometimes, I replied truthfully "She is dead. After all,

Mama, she lived to a ripe old age"; though my grandmother actually died at sixty-four during the hardships of the Second World War. Mama would then look at me and say, "But I am old, too!"

Even in her puzzled state of mind, while questioning me, she would look at me with her large hazel eyes. The eyes whose sweet maternal gaze I knew since childhood and in troubled adult moments when she helped me through crises. She had faced her own crises, the sorrows and trials of her emigration, Papa dying, and said, "You must be strong!" which sustained me and still sustains me through the unpredictable surges of guilt and remorse threatening to undo the hard-earned sane and bright march through the everyday. That gaze, filled with wisdom and love, could not be buried with Mama in her tomb; it transcends ash; it cannot disintegrate into residue.

During my visits to the nursing home, as I prepared to depart, Mama would accompany me to the elevator in her wheelchair. Though her connection to telephones waned, when the elevator arrived and I stepped in, she would cry out, "Three rings, three rings."

Sometimes, when I left the cemetery near twilight, I would look up at the sky and discern the evening star, Venus. Up there, near Venus, I imagined Mama looking down at me. She was waving and calling out, "Three rings, three rings."

When a family member or a friend dies, something dies within us—the way we talked together, the way we laughed together, the time we spent together. Although that person has been erased from the earth, we, still alive, keep that person alive, in memory, in framed photographs, in memoirs. Paradoxically, a little segment of us dies with that person, and that person lives on.

I left the Salisbury pink granite gravestone, reverently monitoring Mama's last domicile, and walking down the hill, I passed the young woman in the draped gown, holding flowers in one hand, and supporting her head with the other. Yes, she was still pensive; she would not, no, never, comprehend the grim jurisdiction of Death, the inexorable finality of extinction, for she was young and beautiful, and youth cannot conceive of the meaning of *to cease* in its mortal sense. I passed the little girl leaning against the flowered rail, still caught up in Alice-in-Wonderland dreams. Oh, stay within those dreams, little girl, for knowledge of your death, so young, so filled with pathos, is hard for the living and perhaps the dead to bear. I passed the mournful seated hooded androgynous figure frozen in the death swoon. Oh, what do you see in your swoon, beautiful statue? Truly, the "pleasant dreams," suggested in William Cullen Bryant's poem, "Thanatopsis"?

For a moment, I paused and looked back to gaze at the funereal stone city. It stood in stoic silence, guarding the enigmatic secrets of death within its immutable stillness.

Part Two

My Father Anton

7

Young Anton in Montevetuso

ONCE AGAIN, these pages traverse the mighty Atlantic, making their circuitous way to that city atop an isolated mountain, revealing its breathtaking panorama. At night, when gazing from the east, one can see the row of lamplights along the esplanade of the Gulf of Taranto. Gazing in other directions, one can see far-off mountains (Italy's hill cities) twinkling with their lights, the lights defining a cupola or a tower or a castle. Surely, this place was the setting for fairy tales, a place which induced dreams of grand scope! And thus it was for my father.

In one of the contiguous houses nestled along a narrow cobblestone street, a house painted in a light ochre shade, lived a little boy, my father, Anton, short for Antonio. Had I stood before that house in the early twentieth century, I would have seen a small grocery store on the first floor, for my paternal grandmother ran a grocery to help support a family with seven children. Her husband, my grandfather, was an artist, crafting sizeable papier-mâché statues of saints to be placed in the various churches to be found along the cobblestone streets, sometimes right next door to a house, for a walled city built on a mountaintop has sparse room for even a mere break between two houses. I would not know how much money my grandfather, Papa's father, might have earned for his artfully crafted statues, ensuring saintly casts of expression, though he might have well considered himself much honored by their being placed in a church and, possibly, being prayed to by those devoted to that saint.

One year Papa's father sent us large, sculpted figures for our crèche. We put these nativity figures in the large paper mâché manger cousin Luigi made for us and placed the scene under our Christmas tree at our home on Eastville Avenue. The crèche included figures of Mary, Joseph, baby Jesus, and oxen, but what I, as a child, was in wonder of was the Christmas angel perched on the roof of the crèche, holding the scroll announcing, Gloria in Excelsis Deo. The angel had large whitish wings faintly interwoven with pinkish and bluish hues, which made them look as soft and as fleecy as feathers. When I touched the wings, it was always a surprise to find them hard, for they were made of papier-mâché. To my delight, I discovered that the angel had deep slots in the back into which the separate wings, constructed with a small round protrusion were fitted. I could slip the wings off and on the perched angel!

Aside from sculpturing angels and saints, to make a living, Papa's father wove baskets and grew and arranged flowers for weddings, baptisms, funerals, and other family festivities. Occasionally, he sent us flower seeds, hinting at his green thumb. Perhaps he owned a small piece of land just outside the city walls for cultivation, but the most readily available spaces were balconies and flat roofs. In the contiguously constructed ancient towns, ingenious uses were made of a flat roof. It was a highly prized space to grow plants and carry out housework. Under Italy's brilliant sun, women dried laundry, figs, tomatoes, and peppers, and might put out a vat to capture rainwater.

I remember coming home one day to find Papa sitting on our sofa chair with one elbow perched on the side and his other hand spread across his forehead, shading his eyes. There, he sat, in deep mourning, for a black-bordered letter had arrived announcing the death of his father.

Like many other families, Anton's family, had been caught up in Southern Italy's endemic *miseria*, though industriously engaged in gainful pursuits to maintain a reasonable standard of living. Anton, the second born child, was an unusually smart boy. He understood the family's struggle, and carried out responsibilities, helping his mother or his father, as needed. When he was about six or seven, one of his responsibilities was to accompany a woman visitor home, for women then did not walk alone, and the woman, knowing the customs of the city, did not think it was unusual to be accompanied by a young boy. The people of the city knew that in their remarkable way, children knew every street and alley and shortcut of the small city compressed on the mountaintop. They were resourceful and agile, and in the event of an accident or assault, they would instantly raise the alarm. Nothing escaped their keen vigilance when it came to unusual occurrences within their city.

Once, in the nineteen fifties, the children saw two women in pants, actually, my sister and I, wearing slacks, not realizing that such an outfit was scandalous at that time in Southern Italy. Not only were we in slacks, but we were also walking unaccompanied! Several children cried out, *uomini! uomini!* (men) and threw little stones at us, which of course did not reach us. The tradition of women being accompanied, whether by young boys or an adult, continued among the older generation through the twentieth century.

The families also knew that Montevetuso had its own surveillance system, which detected any unusual happenings: a system akin to the hundred eyes of Argus. There were eyes on balconies, on flat roofs, through the openings of shutters, behind curtains, and by retired old men in berets sitting hour after hour outside on Piazza Roma. The eyes detected a child, accompanying a woman, and from their different locations, the eyes followed their journey until the woman reached her destination and the child returned home.

In his free time, young Anton, at the age of six or seven, would have ambled about the city and inevitably ended up in the labyrinth—the section of the city that decades later would be referred to as the Historic Center. He would have walked around bends in the tiny streets, into dead ends, climbed up staircases that lead to other tiny streets or down staircases leading to streets on lower levels. Sometimes, over the stairs would be a roof, creating a short suffocating tunnel. Anton would then emerge onto a street that perhaps led to a dead end on the right but an open street on the left.

In his wanderings, he would pass that little Renaissance church with Corinthian columns, barricaded, but probably once a private chapel of nobility; that fountain in the middle of a small piazza, to provide water for women filling their amphoras and bearing them supported on a hip or on their heads to one of the nearby small, sometimes one-room houses.

Perhaps the most captivating sight Anton would behold in the labyrinth, though only by chance, were the women in black: black dresses, black stockings, black shoes, black head kerchiefs, the overwhelming black broken by the flashing of gold earrings. Upon espying one of the women, perhaps just turning a bend, he fancied that the women in black lived in the walls of the labyrinth and were part of the labyrinth's mysterious maze of streets, staircases, and small sheltered passageways.

During his explorations through the labyrinth, young Anton would have undoubtedly encountered a street named Via Giulio Verne. Perhaps he wondered, who was Giulio Verne? Years later, whether through self-learning or a school library, he would learn that Giulio Verne was a French writer who had achieved worldwide fame and was translated into many different languages.

Venturing beyond the dense center of the labyrinth but onto an outlying street paralleling the city walls, he would have come to Via del Sale, the Salt Road. Anton was too young then to realize how historically significant the salt road was, surely as significant as the Silk Road, for how did ancient cities obtain that most precious commodity, salt? (In Germany, it was sometimes referred to as the "white gold" road.) He might even have caught sight of the peddlers on mules carrying sacks of salt. Later, he would learn that the route these merchants took was from the salt flats of the city of Metaponto. The sacks of salt were transported to Montevetuso and then on to Matera, the capital of the province. He would become familiar with the Sali e Tabacchi stores, learning later that they were under government control (some of which today, now selling other goods, still retain the old salt and tobacco signs).

More often than not, young Anton would walk along the main corso, ascending to the top of the mountain. He would pass contiguous grand palatial houses with large iron-wrought balconies patterned with arabesque forms. Here, was the nobility or a wealthy upper class. One particular house, not on the main corso but around the corner, and there, less conspicuous, caught his attention. Anton, perhaps hidden in a dark nook, would observe the occupants stepping in and out of that grand house into the emblazed family coach. He noted their fine clothes, their gestures, their formal bows. He listened to live classical music drifting through the elegantly carved open French doors and surmising that the instrument producing such beautiful sounds might be a piano, though he had never seen one.

Then he made his way back to his modest house and daily routine of chores and play. As in the keen image-absorbing minds of children, he understood that there was this life in the house of his family and there was that life in the grand houses, a life he was not born into. As he grew, that "instruction" of observing the nobility stayed with him, and he would decide that, never mind, he could possess its elegance, its gallantry, its refinement of the senses in another way: he could cultivate them. He could be described as *educato* (in its Italian connotation meaning well-bred, a gentleman). As he matured, he would become aware that his childhood observations of the deportment of the nobility, had become embedded in his subconscious. He found himself making certain gracious gestures or giving a slight bow in a formal context, as an introduction to someone.

As Natalia and I grew up, he emphasized the importance of good manners to us. Occasionally, after a day's work, he would draw our attention to a clip he had saved from *The Daily News* (never the whole newspaper!), featuring Elinor Ames's snippet, *"The Correct Thing,"* offering advice on proper social behavior. We were very attentive to that day's lesson and particularly impressed by the photograph illustrating the proper behavior.

8

The Dream of a Piano

In Montevetuso, basically an agricultural city, there were limited opportunities for boys as young as Anton to earn a few lire, which, as in other cities in Europe, was a primary cause for emigration to America. Anton's family hardly had the finances to send Anton to school to become an elementary school teacher. There was always recourse to the church, entering the priesthood. One of his sisters took that recourse and became a nun. There was always a need for tailors, who were also adept at altering clothes, perhaps adapting a pair of pants for the next growing sibling. A combination of thoughtfulness in relation to the character of their son and work opportunity led Anton's parents to decide to apprentice him to a tailor.

Of tailoring, Charles Lamb wrote, "There is a professional melancholy . . . incident to the occupation of a tailor." Anton, by nature, was a serious and contemplative individual, to which an occupation such as tailoring seemed fitting—hours alone, the arm moving mesmerizingly up and down as he stitched and stitched, hundreds of shining silk stitches, joining cloths to bring suits and coats into form. He became a fine tailor, expert in every aspect of the craft. Among possible trades, what trades could be more fitting to Anton's notions of being *educato*. He would always be dressed in clothes of peerless elegance, which he could never otherwise afford.

Another significant phase of Anton's development into the persona I knew as Papa was his deep connection to music. In Montevetuso, when young Anton heard music, he knew that whatever acoustical vibrations emerged as tones on an instrument or in the human voice also vibrated within him. The brain was complicated, but clearly, sound waves, whether sonorous or dissonant spoke to him, to all his senses. Here, was a language he understood as naturally as he did his own language, Italian.

When Montevetuso's band marched through the narrow cobblestone streets, bearing a saint, as, the patron saint, Saint Rocco, on a float, Anton would follow the marching band. During the lavishly celebrated feast of Saint Rocco, which took place in August, a big bandstand with hundreds of fairy-tale lights was erected on Piazza Roma. When the musicians stopped their band concert for intermission, young boys would climb up and delightedly run around the now emptied bandstand. But Anton did not run around. He would look closely at the scores left on the music stands and see several straight lines and on them strange figures: small round black heads with a stem, like a flower stem, some of them single and some, united with a line beneath them. Some of the single heads were white, and there was another figure, round and fat, no stem. How could the music he heard spring from these incomprehensible round shapes that did not move and were silent?

When in a nearby church, the organist was playing the organ, Anton would be sitting in one of the back rows and listening. That action spelt his destiny. Understanding that the now familiar boy sitting and listening to him loved music, the organist took

Anton under his tutelage. He not only taught him musical notation and how to play the organ but also enrolled him in a school the church provided for boys, teaching basic educational skills and perhaps some Latin.

Yet, Anton longed for another musical instrument, the one he heard through the open French doors of the grand house he would observe as he hid in a nook—a piano. His sparely accommodated school did have several books, and in one of them, about musical instruments, he saw photographs of pianos. There was the upright and a stunning one called a grand piano, certainly the piano owned by the nobility in that fine house. When he grew up, he would buy a piano, an upright, which was luxury enough for him. Perhaps he could start right now to earn some liras to buy a piano when he grew older.

There were few opportunities in Montevetuso for boys as young as Anton to earn a few liras, but he knew of one. During the feasts dedicated to patron saints, like Saint Rocco, other revered saints, and the Madonna, all the church bells would ring with the joy of celebration, including the bells of Montevetuso's grand cathedral with its attached campanile (*la chiesa madre*). The bells were made of iron and were very, very heavy. Anton learned that the priests or laymen in charge reward bell-pulling boys with a few lire, and he resolved that when he grew into fuller boyhood and became stronger, he would volunteer to climb up to the campanile of the cathedral, or any available church, and pull the bell rope back and forth. He would have to start early in the morning to earn those liras, for there was much competition to be a bell ringer. The boys would eagerly scramble up to the bell tower and from there breathlessly behold all of Montevetuso. Then, with great exhilaration, they would pull the bell rope back and forth, back and forth. Yes, he would commence saving for a piano by participating as a bell ringer in one the churches.

Subsequently, imagining that he had transacted payment for

an upright piano, he tried to figure out how his upright piano would be brought up the mountain. Like all the young boys, he was aware of everything pertaining to the everyday activity in Montevetuso. When something heavy, perhaps a piece of furniture, was delivered to Montevetuso, it was drawn up the mountain by horse and carriage. That was how his upright piano would be delivered to him, coming all the way from Naples.

From the city walls, staring hard at the vast panorama, he imagined that far off, he saw a moving speck coming closer. The route was circuitous, and sometimes the speck disappeared from view, only to appear again. As it came nearer, he could make out a carriage driven by two horses, and there, within it, was his piano, protected in layers of heavy cloth. Now it reached the foot of the mountain, and he imagined it being drawn up to where he was standing. Up and up, the straining horses pulled, with the piano occasionally tilting slightly to one side; up and up, the straining horses pulled, with the piano tilting gently to the other side, past those towering cypress trees growing at the side of the mountain. Finally, at the mountain's summit, stood Anton, eagerly awaiting his very own piano.

However, destiny had other plans for Anton, and he would finally own his upright piano on another continent.

9

Musical Life in New York City

ON JULY 17, 1920, at the age of twenty, Anton embarked for America at the port of Naples, on the transatlantic liner, *Patria*. Anton was destined to make the journey between Montevetuso and America three times, starting with the 1920 trip. It is in character that Anton, always aspiring to be *educato* and as a tailor, to be impeccably dressed, would save enough money to travel second-cabin passenger each time. Emigrating to America, many men from Montevetuso perceived their emigration as temporary. Those who returned described their experiences of the journey. The alarming tales of Ellis Island circulated the mountaintop city. Amazingly, despite the expense and the hardships of travel conditions, as well as the consternations of leaving the family (often wife and children), a good number of men made the trip several times. My maternal grandfather made the journey twice.

In 1920, upon stepping onto the actual terra of the dreamed-of New World, Anton first roomed with one or two friends. His fine tailoring skills were recognized, and he quickly found ready employment in an elegant clothes shop on Fifth Avenue, tailoring for such celebrities as French soprano, Lily Pons, and Marlene Dietrich. When he was able to rent his own apartment, he finally fulfilled that childhood dream of owning an upright piano. Throughout my childhood, our various apartments were always resonating with music.

But the saga of pianos in Anton's life could not end with an upright piano. He must go further. The marvelous parts making up a piano, the hammers, the strings, the tuning pins, the pedals, achieved their utmost potentials in creating the piano sound and its amazing variations in volume within a horizontal structure as opposed to an upright structure—the structure of the grand piano. To Papa, to own a grand piano was not only to own a piano in its most elevated form of production but also for its bestowal of status in this ever strange New World, in which besides being an immigrant, he was an immigrant from Southern Italy, not altogether welcome in the New World except as a laborer needed to achieve the goals of the New World's ever-growing metropolises. Yet, besides these solid reasons, owning a grand piano was the continuing fulfillment of the aspirations of the little boy who determined to emulate the nobility and become that *gentilhomme,* that persona looked upon as *educato.*

In 1940, twenty years after his emigration from Italy, Anton, now in his early forties, walked into Hardman, Peck & Co., which in the thirties and forties had a piano showroom in New York City, on Fifty-seventh Street, the same street on which Carnegie Hall was located. Dressed in the finest tailored man's suit to be seen on Manhattan streets, as in a dream, he heard his own voice transacting the monumental (for his budget) purchase of six hundred and ninety dollars, less seventy dollars for his upright piano. Unbelievably, even to himself, he made the leap. Now, the crowning glory of pianos, was his, an ebony baby grand and a bench.

In our house on Eastville Avenue, in the Bronx, Mama,

Natalia, and I gazed in wonder at this ebony majesty, its lid flaring up like the sweep of a giant wing, placed in the corner of our airy eight-windowed parlor. The grand piano seemed to even transform the stature of our first floor four-room apartment, even of us. Now, when our Italian *Schubertiades* took place, evenings of company and music, friends singing opera arias and Neapolitan folk songs, Papa would accompany them on the baby grand. Papa had taught us, his two children, to play the piano, and now we studied our lessons on a baby grand piano! Sometimes, on those evenings, he would perform four-hand piano pieces with us, his favorite choice being Rossini overtures.

There was another site in Manhattan, aside from Fifty-seventh Street, that filled Anton with wonder. That little boy with surely impossible dreams, confined in a walled city that now to him seemed to be more a hallucination than a reality, was here, at this moment, on Union Square, in Manhattan. Anton had a modest collection of musical scores, but he always needed new repertoire pieces, particularly as his daughters advanced in dexterity.

Here he was, standing in the Carl Fischer music store, a twelve-story building on Union Square housing many company offices, a printing press, and millions of musical scores. For musicians, simply entering the building at Cooper Square was like entering another world, their world, a world in which architectures of sound moving through time, compassed the whole range of human emotions. Here, in this sacrosanct place, were the spirits of Beethoven, of Chopin, and perhaps even famous current musical performers and composers, among all the musicians pouring over scores. Detached from the hustle and bustle of traffic and rushing-about people outside, like a world of music, the Carl Fischer store was a sanctuary, and what a temptation to musicians and students to linger, to browse through random scores, to just, as, the phrase was coined, "hang around." And here was Papa, among them, musicians, performing musicians, eager students, in the greatest music store of the great city of New York!

The moderately small-statured, slender man, impeccably dressed, a Southern Italian immigrant from an ancient Southern Italian hill city so far off, yes, astronomically miles away from New York City, was here. He had set off from his birthplace by horse and carriage, carrying him to the train, which transported him to the Port of Naples. There, as if in a dream, he had walked up the gangplank to the great passenger liner, which after sounding its poignant three long foghorns, embarked on its voyage across the mighty Atlantic Ocean. All of this, and now he found himself in the renowned Carl Fischer Music store in the great City of New York.

Were there miracles in life, Anton wondered? Yes, he affirmed, there were.

Carl Fischer closed its store on Union Square in 1999.

10

The Moving Finger

My portrayal of Anton and his early life in Montevetuso and emigration to America was based on my perceptions of his character. Papa had two sides harmoniously fitting together that made up his temperament, the deeply serious thinker with a passion for music and a social bent enjoying a house full of company.

As I noted earlier, quoting Charles Lamb who wrote, "There is a professional melancholy . . . incident to the occupation of a tailor." In nature, Anton was serious and given to deep thought, to which an occupation such as tailoring happened to be fitting.

In our apartment on Eastville Avenue, he had installed a sewing room in a small, unheated room exiting to the back stairs, to make suits for private customers, thereby supplementing his salary, as well as to make all of us suits or coats, according to the season. In winter, he heated the room with a sun lamp, less than two feet high, placed on the floor. Mama would also use the treadle sewing machine to make dresses, blouses, and skirts for us, as well as for herself. Usually, after dinner, held at seven o'clock,

Papa would go to the sewing room, until retiring, at ten o'clock. Who can say what thoughts circulated around his mind. He had ample subjects to dwell upon, all the joys and heartbreaks of two worlds, two continents.

Serious Papa also served as Natalia's and my piano teacher. I have vivid memories of my piano lessons every Saturday morning. Papa would stand beside the grand piano with a pencil in his hand, listening as I played the previous lesson I learned and teaching me the next page, at the end of which he would pencil a scribble, sometimes big and exuberant, sometimes of a mild medium size. In the space at the beginning of the piece, he would pencil a large number—four, six, or eight—indicating how many times to practice the new segment. It was always even numbers, never three, five, or seven. Upon occasion, I would consistently miss hitting the right note, and losing patience, Papa would take my finger and put it pointedly on that key, exclaiming, in Italian, *"mi bemolle! mi bemolle!"* (E flat), which of course did not ease my anxiety as I came upon the next *mi bemolle* in the piece.

Papa was a staunch believer in the importance of technique, and my piano lessons included a rigorous regimen of technical exercises in volumes by Hanon, Czerny, Cementi, and Tausig, but Papa preferred the *Mètodo* of Beniamino Cesi, piano professor at the conservatory of Naples. As a young adolescent, I was captivated by Cesi's stunning handlebar mustache, exhibited in his large portrait in my arpeggio book. Cesi—and the remarkable handlebar mustache—seemed to gaze into the distance, likely not at the Bay of Naples but concocting another convoluted arpeggio to eke out of the poor, sweating piano keys. Perhaps the crowning exercise book was Clementi's *Gradus ad Parnassum,* for completing Clementi's "Steps to Parnassum," I would sit alongside the Muses on Mount Parnassus.

As previously mentioned, we had a foot-pumped harmonium placed near the baby grand piano. Papa had bought that harmonium several years after he bought the baby grand. Perhaps its reedy organ sound brought back memories of the little boy whose first lessons on a keyboard were on the organ. Or, perhaps its reedy organ sound brought him closer to that pastoral feel of Italy, of Montevetuso itself, as he might have felt when he played the shepherd's lively bagpipe song at Christmastime. Whatever the inspiration, the little four-octave harmonium became literally instrumental in my development as a pianist. With the frenzy of technique, technique, technique, I had developed a technique quite at the level of a virtuosic pianist, and it was time to learn concertos. The humble little harmonium became my orchestra. Papa would go to Carl Fischer Music on Cooper Square, and buy two copies of each concerto, scored for two pianos. With great skill, he would reduce the piano score arranged for eighty-eight keys into a score for thirty-two keys. And so, sounding through the four rooms of our apartment on Eastville Avenue were the concertos of Tchaikovsky, Liszt, Grieg, and Rachmaninoff, with papa furiously pumping away on the foot pedals, lest I lose my orchestra.

In my yearbook album, when I graduated from the eighth grade, Papa wrote,

I want you healthy
I want you good!
I want you <u>Happy</u> (Papa's underline)
Honest and True—
You can make me
Happy too; by playing
<u>The Piano</u> (Papa's underline)
Your life trough! [writing the word as he pronounced it]
Father

I continued to play the piano throughout my life, and now, in old age, its significance to me has grown even stronger. Apart from helping maintain agility in my fingers, it provides structure to the swiftly passing amorphous run of days and keeps my emotions in good working order, feeling the passions of fortissimos and the contemplative strains of pianissimos.

Nostalgically, I revisit those moments now—me at the piano, playing with a daredevil energy, an almost runaway dazzle of technique and strength, and Papa pumping and pumping to keep the music sounding, sounding through the decades, into the twenty-first century.

Aside from the serious side, there was also the social Papa, who relished having a house full of company. Papa was a man with a flair, an air, always the master of ceremonies. He had a Roman profile (a feature of Papa's paternal family I inherited) and his gray hair, which though growing sparser in front, bushed back, like arpeggios sweeping from the bottom of the piano to the treble. There was still an aura about him that might have fleetingly summoned up an image of the then-current actor, John Barrymore.

Had he not, in those 1920 days, danced that most seductive and captivating urban Argentine dance electrifying the ballrooms of Europe—the tango! He had seen and been enchanted by Rudolph Valentino in the American film, *The Four Horsemen of the Apocalypse.*

During our musical nights, our Italian Schubertiads, he was not just the master of ceremonies but also the master, the maestro. As he accompanied singers, he would prompt one of them who often forgot the words of a piece; he could transpose a key higher or lower with little effort to accommodate a singer; and sometimes, as when two singers performed a duo, he would lift his left hand from the piano and conduct them to a final, resounding fortissimo.

Our musical nights were usually followed by Mama's *spuntino* (snack), which Mama magically laid out on the large kitchen table within minutes: roasted peppers, pepperoni, olives, provolone cheese, artichoke hearts, the authentically made crusty Italian bread, and wine. Looking at the festive table and gathering as a genre painting, one would see the men dressed in suits and ties and the women in Sunday dress, probably corseted as needed or contained in the more merciful girdles.

In our era, as adults, we were more formal, dressing up for occasions that were simply outings of the everyday. For women, corsets or the less confining, more flexible girdles; garter belts, to hold up long stockings; and sanitary belts to hold up sanitary pads were all part of everyday dress. With all the encumbrance of underwear in that era, it would have been impossible to don the currently tight and smoothly fitting leggings! One good friend of our family donned hat, gloves, and heeled shoes to shop at the local stores. My cousin upstairs, Luigi, who planted his front garden with dahlias of all sizes, in bright, solid, and variegated colors, donned suit, tie, and fedora to visit a dahlia farm to buy new brands of dahlias, as did his grown son, who drove him to the farm. No adults wore sneakers, even for casual wear. In winters, fedoras were still the proper style to be worn by men, though they did not cover the ears. Afflicted with ear problems, Papa would insert cotton soaked in warmed olive oil into his ears. In that era, it would have been unthinkable to sensibly wear a wool cap.

If in that genre painting, one could hear the voices in genial conversation, one would hear, "Yes, yes, Mr. Rossi, I agree!" or "Like you, Mr. Amati, I had the same experience." Although here was a group of close friends of long acquaintance, men called one another by Mister and surname, and they called women, Signora, or Signorina. In the early stages of friendship, women also used the formal address of Missus and surname, but as the relations between women became closer, women addressed each other by given names. Children, of course, used the titles, Mister and

Missus. I remember the surnames of our family's friends, but either forgot or never knew the given names.

By the time he reached his fifties, Papa was well established in the New World and had surrounded himself with close friends. Of course, always looming in his consciousness was Montevetuso, high on the mountain, where his childhood family resided. There, was his *true* home. Nonetheless, there were good, fulfilling years he could look ahead to in the New World.

Our cousins who lived upstairs, made wine every year in the cellar for their family and for Papa, who would order his share of boxes of select grapes, according to his particular formula. In a black and white photograph capturing the wine making process, father and son, joined by Papa, are holding a long metal handle elongated by an attached rod--three men at the press, walking round and round to squeeze out the last drops of the crushed grapes. The three men are smiling and looking into the camera. My cousins are wearing a plaid jacket, and Papa is wearing a dark silky bathrobe! Probably, he had been chatting with them and then joined them to pose for the photograph. That silky bathrobe in the milieu of a winemaking scene, however impromptu, conveyed something in character with Papa, that flair, that making more of a moment, creating a bit of drama, placing the moment on stage.

Every year on New Year's Day, Papa would carry his gallon of new wine in a cloth bag and walk several blocks to visit his friends to wish them a happy New Year, baptized, as it were, by the new wine, particularly personal because the wine was made according to his formula. It was, after all, in his eyes a significant moment, as was any that pertained to cementing friendship, and he dressed accordingly.

He'd don his meticulously crafted dark gray winter coat, which, of course, he made, as he did all our winter coats. The coat featured fastidiously turned lapels that complemented his fedora, a

Homburg, tilted at a smart angle. Under the coat, he would wear his own finely tailored suit and a wingtip collar, which aptly displayed his choice, patterned Italian silk tie, encircling his neck. Even when Papa held New Year's Eve at home, inviting the usual family friends, he wore that formal attire, including the wingtip collar, a style that evolved in the nineteenth century. It was not surprising that when Papa contracted ulcers and was told not to smoke, he cut his cigarettes in half and placed the half in a cigarette holder (as the current president, President Roosevelt, did). The holder may well have cut the number of cigarettes he smoked, but it seemed to go very well with a fine coat and Homburg hat and that ultra-formal wingtip collar.

As he reached our friend's house and rang the bell, I could hear him greeting the signora, who opened the door, "Buon giorno, Signora, buon giorno," and as he was led into the parlor, "Buon anno! Buon anno."

In those years during autumn, I recall the cellar having a grapey scent. In one corner, the metamorphosing grapes would patiently age in oak barrels to eventually mature in time to herald in the next New Year.

With time, as circumstances in both families, both our cousins and ours, changed, the quaint custom of hailing the New Year with homemade wine turned into a cherished memory—a solacing memory for Papa, warmed by the heartening knowledge that he had many friends. Today, in a storage room, the nearly century-old wine press, with parts of its light wooden verticals stained a dark brown, still awaits that heavy, earthy smell of matured grapes to be loaded into its basket to be transformed into a liquid for Papa's New Year's gift of a gallon of new wine and his yearly greeting, "Buon anno! Buon anno!"

As 1942 gave way to the 1950s, new trends in daily life began to emerge. Families were beginning to dine out! Why, yes, thought Papa, he and Annina could choose a nice restaurant and occasionally dine out. He and Annina might even take a little vacation, somewhere nearby, for not having a car, they would travel by train or bus. They could choose a picturesque town in Westchester County, adjacent to the Bronx.

Papa felt a sense of upliftment, a relief from the challenges of the immigrant life he had led. By now, he had established a secure life in America, mitigating that ever-insecure feeling of the immigrant in a foreign country, and the new decade, the fifties, promised some diverting activities. There was something else that was taking place right then that filled him with overwhelming joy: his two daughters, Natalia and Annalisa were in college!

Initially, he hadn't been familiar with the word, "college," but later as he learned its meaning, he construed it as a sort of European gymnasium. Whatever it was, Papa felt it was not a social institution that was available to him within the confines of his basic, though good and solid life in America. But it was! To Papa, Anton the immigrant, this was the apex of all that was possible to achieve in America. The light of that torch, out on the New York Bay, held high, had reached his house, on Eastville Avenue.

Papa nostalgically recalled a time when his two daughters were little. During summers, as they spotted him up the block on his way home from work, they would run up to him to greet him and kiss him. Then, how precious were those moments when hand in hand, they walked down the block together, home to dinner. And he recalled how on some nights, as he sewed in his small workshop, his daughters would stand at the door and listen as, in installments, he told them the story of poor Cosette and Jean Valjean, in Victor Hugo's novel, *Les Misérable*. (Natalia and I were rapt by the story but probably as much by the rhythm of Papa's accompanying hand, moving up and down, up and down, as he sewed his even and lustrous silk stitches.)

In our household, the year nineteen fifty-six held historical significance. In June, Natalia was graduating from college, and I, from a university after four years of postgraduate studies. Natalia's June graduation ceremony took place outdoors, and Papa and Mama proudly attended. Papa, now without his Homburg, wore a Panama Hat. Life in America seemed to promise cheerful conclusions.

Yet, as Omar Khayyám aptly writes, "The Moving finger writes, and, having writ, / Moves on: nor all thy Piety nor Wit, / Shall turn it back to cancel half a Line, / Nor all thy Tears wash out a Word of it."

During those happy days, our family experienced fruitions an immigrant family could hardly hope to achieve. We owned a baby grand piano; Anton and Aninna's two daughters now held college degrees; and they themselves could enjoy a more relaxed life, after enduring the trying perplexities and tensions of the immigrant acclimating to the New World. But "The Moving finger writes, and, having writ, / Moves on."

Two months after Natalia's college graduation, at the age of fifty-six, Papa died suddenly of a fatal heart attack.

Some distance from Eastville Avenue, stands the Bronx Whitestone Bridge, connecting Throggs Neck, in the Bronx, with Whitestone, in Queens. The towers, artfully simple in their rounded art deco design, thrust three hundred and seventy-seven feet skyward, and are flanked on each side by rows of steel girders. The skyward towers overlook the surrounding area and a cemetery not very far off. Papa rests in that cemetery, under the aegis of the great Bronx Whitestone Bridge.

Part Three

My Childhood in the Bronx

11

Eastville Avenue and Life on the City Block

EASTVILLE AVENUE, off Gun Hill Road, in the East Bronx, was in a quiet, residential area. In the 1930s and the 1940s, seven two-story houses of brick and stucco were situated on one side, and five on the other. Yards with towering maple and oak trees were stretched between the houses. One of the seven houses, a fine, pre-World War II brick house, with three porches, two on the first level, and an unroofed porch on the upper level, glows in my memory, as if the brick, suffused with light, were liquid. That house was my childhood house, now unrecognizable beneath a gray vinyl siding and plastic green awnings.

Today, Eastville Avenue, along with other once idyllic avenues in the East Bronx, is lined with houses. Occasionally, a solitary tree in front of a house or off to the side valiantly evokes the lush woodlots that once nurtured us, singling out the seasons of the year.

We called the woods, "the lots." Through May, the woods were sprinkled with dainty white mayflowers, which, as was our school's custom, we picked and brought to school on the first of

May. We hung a paper basket filled with the mayflowers on the doorknobs of classrooms, as a celebration of spring. Later, I learned that our yearly custom commemorated the ancient European festival centered on the maypole. In autumn, we'd roam the woods, collecting the brilliantly colored leaves of maple, oak, and staghorn sumac trees and flattened them in our scrapbooks. In winter, when we had snow, we sleighed in one of the block's woods, which had a sharply descending path, and we ice skated on an ice pond in the deep woods, but a half a block away.

Behind our house, there was another "lot." It served as a shortcut for me when I ran errands for Mama to the local stores. I would playfully skip over a line of boulders, hopping from one to the other. Once, I looked up at a towering tree and looking high up, I saw giant orange and yellow flowers, pictured against the blue sky. I felt as if that tree were in a fairy tale. I learned later that the fairy tale tree was the tulip tree. Perhaps it was from that tree that I would hear a bird's pristine flute-like call on summer dawns, which I later identified as the lilting three-note allegretto of the wood thrush, usually three notes varying in pitch.

One could say that we, the children on the block, had two homes, one, a roofed building, the house of our family, the other, roofed by the sky, the city block. We rarely left our second home. Most of the ten or so children from the neighborhood had immigrant parents from Western Europe or grandparents living with them. No one had bicycles, and no one stayed at school for extracurricular activities, because they did not exist. Perhaps children could play in the schoolyard after school, but we lived in the most outlying district of the school, and once home, after school hours, could give no thought to returning that same afternoon. In summer, no one went to camp, for our immigrant parents and we, the children, did not know of camps, and even if our parents did, they could not afford such expense and having no automobile, could not transport us to a camp or anywhere.

Living essentially on the block, and as children always seeking play or some activity, we identified strongly with the changing seasons. Autumn, as I noted earlier, meant creating scrapbooks with the gold and red leaves from our own woods, and winter meant sledding and ice skating within our own environment. Of course, the greatest seasons for play were spring and summer when we transformed all the block's features into a playground for games.

We were well-acquainted with the 1930s and 1940s sidewalks, featuring seamed five-by-five squares. Ritually, we stepped on the seam because as we learned, or rather, as folklore instructed us, "Step on a crack and break the devil's back."

The rage of that day was to own a high-bouncing pink ball we called a "spaldeen," a local pronunciation of Spalding, a sporting goods company. With the coveted spaldeen, we played box ball, utilizing two sidewalk squares as a field and the seam as a net. We played stoop ball (not knowing that we were using a Dutch word to name staircases leading to a porch or the entrance to a house). My stoop included eight concrete steps. Standing as good a distance from the stoop as we could, without falling off the curb into the street, we threw the ball between the steps of the stoop, the challenge being to throw the ball in a certain way to hit the proper place between the steps and then to catch it on the rebound. Stoop ball, however, was a boy's game, as was the proverbial New York City game, stickball, played in the street with a broomstick or some such and the indispensable spaldeen. Traffic was sparse, for few families had cars, and sometimes my friend Helina and I, along with several other girls, also on the block, played punch ball in the street, punching the spaldeen, palm forward, and following rules pertaining to bases, similar to stickball.

Spring heralded the arrival of hopscotch, called "potsy," on our block, jump rope and bounce ball recitations, marbles, jacks, pick-up sticks, and roller skating noisily up and down the block. Our ball-bearing skates, with steel wheels and heavy ties, were buckled over our oxfords, and when the fit loosened, we readjusted the skate to the shoe with a skate key.

Although we continued to play some of our springtime games in summer, Helina and I had spacious backyards where we could play summertime games. Both of us had pergolas furnished with a table and a long bench. Our pergola produced concord grapes with which Mama made grape jelly. In Helina's backyard, I recall a large pear tree with matured pears ready to be picked and nearby, a small pen with chicks, which Helina's father bought at Easter.

During those long summers, board games were very popular. On long summer afternoons, Helina and I would sit in her pergola and play board games such as checkers or Chinese checkers, but both of us were more drawn into the new, exciting game of Monopoly, placed on the market in 1935. We could identify with its realistic city features, greenhouses, red hotels, railroads, even a jail, and we were intrigued by the adult feel of transacting sales, according to the currency we had in hand.

Occasionally, in my yard, I would set up a croquet game under the two pin oaks. In the evenings, cousin Luigi, who lived upstairs, would organize a bocce game for friends and neighbors. Sometimes, after a game or two, we simply sat on my stoop. We never thought of ourselves as *bored*. We never used the word. We had not heard that word in our houses, where, in any case, our immigrant parents may not have known the word in English or had no cause to use it, always being occupied with practical matters pertaining to daily living and adjusting to New World usages.

We were perfectly content sitting on the stoop of our second home. Not having automobiles in the family or scheduled lessons off the block, time moved slowly for us. In my childhood schooldays, the lapse of time between the end of June and the beginning of September was a stretch of land as endless as the Sahara. The distance from one Christmas, a peak in the year like the Himalayas, to another was the distance from Eastville Avenue to the city of Oz: eons of time and long journeys through play hours, practicing-the-piano hours, schooldays, and Sunday pasta-and-meat-sauce dinners. Even the Sundays seemed separated by a good several miles from the other. However, as we sat on the stoop, there was one schedule for me, piano practice at five o'clock, when, usually, I waited for Mama to call me.

Among those 1940s seasonal activities was a ritual Natalia and I engaged in on summer evenings. At about seven o'clock, just before dinnertime, we'd stand in front of our house and look up the block, awaiting Papa. Recognizing his distinctive flecked white suit or blue jacket and white pants—a two-tone suit—we knew it was Papa and would run up the block to greet him and kiss him. He would take each of us by the hand and walk down the block, past the differently styled one-and-two storied houses, brick and stucco, interspersed with wooded lots with oak and maples trees, to our house with its concrete stoop.

Considering Papa's reflective nature, I know that our little promenade together represented precious moments in his demanding workdays as a tailor. For us, they were the small, unsung moments that brightened our daily lives —moments that never found their place in the family album but in the recesses of memory.

In 1937, breaking our daily summer game routines, there was an exciting new recreational opportunity drawing us out of the confines of the length and width of the block. Orchard Beach, the Bronx's sole public beach, opened to the public. The impressive new beach, with softly giving whitish sand, free bathhouses, lockers, and athletic fields, was nicely landscaped with flowers, shrubs, and various genera of trees. The expansion of the original small Orchard Beach was largely due to the efforts of New York City's Park Commissioner Robert Moses.

When I was about ten years old and Natalia, seven, Mama had been in America for only ten years, and she was still the immigrant becoming accustomed to American ways and learning basic everyday English, aided later by attending night school. Yet, at that time, she did not yet feel wholly comfortable taking a bus, even more so with her two children, or asking for information or transfers to other buses. But always enterprising, on a summer day, she would pack a blanket and our lunches—typically, an omelet or hard-boiled eggs, contained within Italian bread (the widely advertised Bond Bread never entered our cuisine) and fruit—into a cloth bag, have us put on our bathing suits beneath our dresses, and take us to Orchard Beach. Mama must have heard about this new public beach from friends, though it is hard to imagine how she knew the complicated way to get there.

With our blanket, towels, and lunches, we would walk up the block to Gun Hill Road and board the Gun Hill Road bus to (perhaps) Hutchinson River Parkway, where with bus transfers, we took another bus. As a child, I was not cognizant of the route and bus lines we took, but as we traveled toward our destination, we traversed a bridge with tall towers on either side, which I later learned was the Pelham Bridge. I would look forward to seeing the bridge and traversing it, since for us, the children virtually living solely on the block, seeing a bridge, a real bridge was a wonder. I recall that on one particular trip, the bus stopped at the head of the bridge, and to my unbelieving eyes, the bridge floor slowly rose, higher and higher, until all I saw before my eyes was this huge vertical black structure blocking any view beyond it, and to me, almost frightening. As I learned later, the bridge was a drawbridge —a bascule bridge--opening to allow tall watercraft passage.

I'm not certain if Mama was as surprised at this startling movable bridge floor as I, for probably during her life in Italy, she had been to the city of Taranto, located on the Gulf of Taranto, and was aware of the *Ponte Girevole* (the swinging bridge), a landmark on the Gulf. Rather than moving upward into a vertical position like the Pelham Bridge, the two halves of the bridge roadway swing sideways toward the embankment and position themselves parallel to it. This opening allowed for watercraft passage through the canal.

Once on the beach, Mama spread the blanket, and in our bathing suits, we ran into water, prancing around and splashing about gleefully. We did not know how to swim, nor did Mama who might have simply bathed her feet and legs in the invigorating salt water. We knew nothing about lockers or bathhouses, and Mama could not take two busses home with a wet bathing suit under her dress.

Perhaps as Mama stood in the salt water, relishing the rhythm and the white frothy cascades falling from the cresting of the waves, her thoughts traveled to Italy and her family. No one knew how to swim but, if or when possible, all would travel to the ocean, believing that salt in the ocean was salutary to health, remedial for those afflicted with rheumatism or arthritis, or simply healthy, as healthy as vitamin D from the sun.

Eating our lunch on a blanket in the sand was part of the novelty of a day at Orchard Beach. Occasionally, as we savored our sandwiches, we'd hear a distant siren, and looking toward the spacious boardwalk, we'd see an ambulance. Someone on the beach, lying prostrate, was stricken with sunstroke.

At about three in the afternoon, Mama packed the blanket, towels, and other picnic utensils in her cloth bag, and we set off for our journey back home, our bathing suits almost dry under our dresses. Two buses, the Pelham Bridge, Gun Hill Road, and then the walk down the block to our brick house brought that exceptional day away from the city block to an end.

While the beach outings were highly memorable occasions,

the simple street games provided us with both pleasure and were a source of learning. Ours was an era when poetry and the sheer simple enjoyment of reciting rhymed lines was part of street games. At school, we had to memorize poems, and sometimes, which we dreaded, we had to recite the poem in an Assembly program. It was alarming enough to recite the poem in front of the class and our classmates. We learned the poems by rote, which occasionally failed us, and we stumbled or lost concentration.

Yet, on the city block, we, at least, the girls, memorized verse after verse of the recitations constituting part of our bounce ball and jump rope games. How did I learn all those verses? I knew them as if spontaneously, as if the lore of children's street games were imbedded in the street, in the sidewalks, in the neighborly air, as if the voices of children of past generations reached us and indoctrinated us. Nor in the mental stance of playing games, boys in their games, girls, in theirs, was there a moment's loss of concentration or stumbling. The memorization, concentration, and the coordination of physical activity exacted by the traditional children's street games constituted a natural schooling for us. The "undivided attention" teachers sought from their students during class lessons was to be found right here, on Eastville Avenue or any neighborhood city block in the decades when street games were common, and learning was carried on in the context of play.

The bounce ball game included a recitation whose keywords, a noun, signaled raising a leg to pass the ball under it. Failing this quick agile movement and losing control of the ball constituted an "out"—out of the game. The ball must keep bouncing, though sometimes it sidled away, dropping to a feeble bounce. In our dresses or skirts, we would follow it frantically, still reciting, and bounce it madly to generate its spring and prepare for the next leg turn. One or two of our bounce ball recitations ran through the alphabet, for example: "A, my name is Anna: I come from Alabama: My husband's name is Albert;

And we sell apples." We then continued with *B, C,* and onward, until we were "out." Despite the seemingly dull and repetitive nature of these verses, we were held by the challenge of coordinating recitation with raising our leg high enough for the passage of the ball under it. We did not look critically upon the recitations we inherited through street lore. Intuitively, perhaps, we understood that they had the weight of centuries behind them and in substance could well reflect the caprices or whims of folk tales.

In another popular *A*-through-*Z* bounce ball game we played, we gave no thought to the sheer nonsense of the verse: "Once an apple met an apple: Said the apple to the apple; Why the apple don't the apple; Get the apple out of here." Considering this verse, today, I cannot imagine who put these inane lines together and that the verse attained permanence in our bounce ball repertoire. One possible objective of the verse is that each line, except the last, contains the word, "apple," twice, which would require two leg turns per line, right leg and then left, demanding greater skill from us and quick responses. One short bounce ball recitation, memorable because of its ringing rhymes, felt more personal to us because of its combination of familiar events to make up a rhyme: "One, two, three, a-nation; I received my Confirmation; On the day of Decoration; One, two, three, a-nation."

Another cherished form of play in neighborhoods on a city block and on Eastville Avenue was jump rope, short-length ropes for a single player and longer lengths for groups. We jumped to the widely known Teddy Bear verses, originating from President Theodore Roosevelt's era and derived from his bear hunt adventure. We instruct Teddy Bear to perform different actions, turn around, touch the ground, go upstairs, say his prayers, turn out the light, and then, 'Teddy Bear, good-night, good night, good night." The rhymed words are repeated three times, exacting, that we, while jumping, repeat the action three times. We tended to play what was called, "double Dutch," requiring greater skill, less frequently.

The two other jump rope recitations we curiously latched onto our block boarded on black comedy, a genre not unusual for the vagaries of folk imagination.

"Rin Tin Tin / Swallowed a pin; / Went to the doctor; / The doctor wasn't in. / He knocked on the door; / Fell on the floor; / And that was the end of / Rin Tin Tin."

We did not care about poor Rin Tin Tin. We concentrated wholly on jumping over that descending rope and not be *out*. As relatively uninformed children, we never questioned whether our Rin Tin Tin, who died so ingloriously in our recitation, had any relation to the famous German Shepherd dog, Rin Tin Tin. We might not even have known of the existence of Rin Tin Tin. The famous story of Rin Tin Tin was fairly contemporaneous with us (Rin Tin Tin died of pneumonia, in 1932), and possibly the catching, rhythmic name was still ricocheting through the city blocks. In the current spirit of the times, in which poetry fell naturally, aptly, into place in children's play, a poem may have sprouted up around the sing-song name, which lent itself easily to rhyme. Why we did away with poor Rin Tin Tin might be attributed simply to the satisfactory fit of perfect rhymes.

Our other customary rhyme emerged from that same deep psychology of folklore, with its atavistic touch: the cantankerous mothers and the dirty old man. "My mother, your mother / Lived across the way: / Three sixteen, East Broadway. / Each night they had a fight, / And this is what they'd say: / 'Your old man is a dirty old man; / He washes his face with a frying pan; / He combs his hair with the leg of a chair; / Your old man is a dirty old man." In our innocence, we were unaware of the sexual connotations of a dirty old man and simply thought the man was dirty. The cranky mothers and their outrageous accusations probably echoed the adverse traditions about mothers in children's literature.

Eventually, these cross or cruel mothers transformed into the more familiar figure of the wicked stepmother.

As for sexual connotations, in our era, when the subject of sex was not open to discussion or instruction, sex entered street lore and the glee in forming rhymes. One day, as several girls and I stood near our school, a schoolboy, about our age. came up to us, and adopting a leering look, recited: "I received a proclamation/ From the Board of Education / To increase the population / Of the future generation. / Do you want a demonstration?"

Several girls tittered and looked knowingly at one another, but I had no idea of the import of the verse, aside from learning that the Board of Education wanted to increase the population of the future generation. Most likely, the schoolboy himself, with his put-on wicked look, had but a vague idea of the implications of the recitation. Yet, as with street-learned recitations, this clever recitation was instructive. In daily, ordinary speech that schoolboy would never use such words as, "proclamation," "generation," "demonstration."

Playing games on our city block unexpectedly became a steadfast custom during the long summer evenings. Neighbors would sit on porches, and Papa might sit at the piano and play a Chopin nocturne. Cousin Luigi, standing on a ladder, tended to his tall dahlias in the front garden, their colorful open faces greeting passersby. The children on the block, boys and girls, would gather at the upper end of the block where there were no houses and there was a long stretch of sidewalk. One side of the sidewalk was bordered by staghorn sumac trees, brilliant red in autumn. The opposite sidewalk was bordered by a grassy treeless lot. Here, the shrill voices of the children and lower voices of older youth called out the names of games they would play on a street where there was virtually no traffic.

Natalia and I would join them, and together, would run through all the classic street games: Ring-a-levio, Red Rover, Red

Rover; Red Light, Green Light; Giant Steps, with its merry singspiel of steps. Almost inevitably, one figure lurked on the sidelines ready to haunt children's games as well as fairy tales: Old Mother Witch, who appears in a tag game, touching upon the enigmatic relation between mother and children, harking back to folklore. The witch is bent over and walks with a stick. The children recite, "Old mother witch / Couldn't sew a stitch. / Picked up a penny, / And thought she was rich." The witch turns around and faces the children: "Are you my children? "Yes!" reply the cunning children. The question is repeated several times, until with great glee, the children reply, "No!" and run off chased by the witch. The child tagged is the next witch.

Apart from the enigmatic figure of Mother Witch in our games, there was another mysterious character: *It*. *It* was both victim and victor. Did this figure evolve from folklore or myth? Whatever the origin, *It* was a prominent character in our games.

The last house on my side of the block, just before the area where we played our games, belonged to the Siegles. Mrs. Siegle, a kindly woman, talked with an accent, as did most adults on the block except Mrs. Roberts. We were accustomed to hearing *w*'s pronounced as *v*'s; *th*'s pronounced as *d*'s, and hearing the Italian lady who lived on the floor above the Siegles, add an *a* to the end of words, for in the Italian language, words generally end with a vowel.

On those idyllic summer evenings, Mrs. Siegle would laboriously support her husband and slowly help him out of the front door onto the stoop, where she sat him comfortably on the top step. He was a familiar figure to the children, and particularly to Natalia and me, for we passed the house on our way to join the other children for games. In his trembling handheld close to his mouth, was a large white handkerchief to catch the continuous trickle of saliva issuing from his slightly open mouth. His left hand rested immobile on his lap. His head was turned toward the children at the games site. Looking back at him, I saw that his eyes were live and lighted. They were fixed on the children, waiting for them to start their games.

As the summer evening gave onto twilight and the first star, the Evening Star, we trooped home to the chirping of crickets and the flashing of fireflies in our woods. Up at the end of the block, Mrs. Siegle helped her husband stand and guided him up that final step into the house. Tomorrow evening, when the children gather again at the end of the block, he will watch the children play their games, and his eyes will be live and lighted.

12

The World of Fordham Road

LIVING, as we did, contained within our city block, I still recall the excitement I felt on the days we set out for Fordham Road and its environs. Among the scenes immediately surging up in my memory, black and towering, always having the flavor of a surprise, was the incredible Third Avenue Elevated, called the Third Avenue El. I recall myself as a young woman with a shoulder strap pocketbook, wearing pumps with an inch or so heel height, the so-called, "college heel," following the Third Avenue El. I remember its soaring tracks and evenly interspersed columns on my right or left side (depending on my errand) and suddenly hearing a thunderous roar overhead as the train speeded by.

The Third Avenue El eventually came to be viewed as a blight on the communities it passed through and became obsolete. Parts of the El were later demolished, as subways were built. The El, a strikingly bizarre structure running through staid communities, was frequently used as a background in movies, one of the most famous scenes occurring in *The Lost Weekend,* 1947, starring Ray Milland, who played as a drunk.

In 1868, when the elevated train was first proposed, New Yorkers were certain that it would plunge to the street below. Although the El made its runs safely, initially the trains were undependable, frequently jamming between stations, and compelling passengers to descend to the street via hastily erected ladders. One accident occurred in 1929 when two El trains collided, about fifty-five feet above the street, killing one passenger. Aside from their "unsightliness," and the lowered real estate values of streets they ran through, the El, as I recall in my daily use of it, entering at the Gun Hill and White Plains Road station, offered a tour of New York City not available in the supplanting subways, running in various depths under the city.

I remember an unforgettable little scary story that took place for me in relation to the Third Avenue El stop on Castle Hill Avenue—no! Papa, Mama, Natalia, and I did not have to climb down many feet on a hastily erected ladder because our train jammed.

Occasionally, our family would gather for dinner at our cousin Amelia's apartment, located in the Castle Hill District of the Bronx. Amelia's apartment was on the fourth floor of a building parallel to the elevated El train line. Except that just at the corner of Amelia's building, the line turned, the tracks seemingly coming closer to the building and Amelia's corner apartment.

One evening, when we had dinner at Amelia's apartment, I, a child then, looked out of the parlor window into the now darkened New York City night. Suddenly, a series of illuminated train cars came into view, one after another, and were turning frighteningly close to the corner of Amelia's apartment. It seemed to my young eyes almost as if the train would plunge right into the parlor, like a huge dragon. As frightening, or to a child, as spooky, were faces staring into the night-lit windows of buildings, perhaps into Amelia's living room and at me! I jumped back, as if to run away from the dragon train and the staring eyes, but then the train disappeared. With a child's thrill at returning to view again an object that both fascinates and frightens it, I sneaked back to the window and waited for the dragon train to return, but then the visit was over, and we said goodbye to Amelia.

Although the child Annalisa never saw the dragon train again, it lingers in my memory to this day for I still see it, making that turn around the corner of Amelia's apartment. As a child, I might have had feelings about those staring faces I saw but of course could not decipher them. Today, those staring faces in the yellowish light summon up within me a sense of human loneliness, the staring faces passing, passing, as if toward the end of their life, each human being basically alone in an incomprehensible universe. They carry the weight of that poignant loneliness captured in Edward Hopper's paintings of city scenes or in Giorgio de Chirico's *Melancholy and Mystery of a Street*, with its existential sense of humanity stranded in an indifferent universe and the ambivalent meaningfulness or meaninglessness of the little girl rolling a hoop up the lonely street.

In addition to the Third Avenue El were the trolley cars. I felt a particular delight in stepping up into a trolley car. I did not feel the nauseous sensations of carsickness in a trolley as I did in a bus, and would later in a car, when I rode in one. Perhaps the main reason why I looked forward to a trolley ride was that it did make all the cheerful sounds that would be replicated in "The Trolley Song." "Clang, clang, clang went the trolley," sang Judy Garland, in *Meet Me in Saint Louis*. Even now, some seventy or so years later, I still hear that slightly out-of-tune clang, clang, clang, of the trolley. And, yes, the ever-chatty trolleys made other noises too, as in the song: "Ding, ding, ding went the bell," "Chug, chug, chug went the motor," "Buzz, buzz, buzz, went the buzzer." In some trolleys, in the summertime, the side window sashes could be removed, and welcoming fresh air would cool passengers as the trolley's steel wheels made their way along the metal track.

Mama, Natalia, and I would take the Webster Avenue trolley line to go to Fordham Road, a popular section of the West Bronx filled with stores not available in local neighborhoods. It was also home to the celebrated Bronx sites, including Fordham University, an academically excellent, high-ranking Catholic University. Fordham Road was our Fifth Avenue, and the adjacent Grand concourse area was our elite Park Avenue. Located within Fordham's Road environs, on East 187 Street, was Arthur Avenue, site of the Little Italy of the Bronx, where customers bought ricotta and mozzarella made on the premises. The pastry shop made classic Italians pastry such as the *sfogliatella,* a type of flakey phyllo dough, stuffed with ricotta cheese, traditionally known as a Neapolitan specialty. The Sicilian specialty was the *cannolo,* and as with many products of Sicily, attributed in origin to Arabic people, the Muslim Emirate.

Nearby, was the renowned Italian bread bakery, always bustling with customers. One could scarcely reach home without breaking off a piece of the large round thickly crusted bread and bite into the springy, zestful taste of pure, unadulterated baked hard wheat flour. That particular bakery also delivered bread in the local area.

Our local Italian bakery also made good-sized round loaves that Mama would buy. To cut me a slice of bread, she would put the whole loaf against her chest, and using a long wicked-looking bread knife, she would cut across the bread. Observing her, I was sure she would cut right through her chest and behead herself. But no, Mama handed me a good slice of bread, and she was still intact, head and all.

On Fordham Road, our equivalent of Bloomingdale's, catering to a lower-income clientele, was the popular Alexander's department store where they offered attractive clothing, likely imitating more expensive fashions, at affordable prices, such as my woolen "little black dress." Our Macy's was Roger's Department Store, in which we bought my white ice skates. Later, Roger's became Sear's Department Store.

Fordham Road was also the location of Fordham Hospital, the first public hospital in the Bronx. My own memory of the hospital was of a large room, filled with many beds, where (as advised by the medical profession, for the benefit of children's health), I had my tonsils and adenoids removed. I still recall the mask, placed over my lower face and breathing in a dense repulsive smell —ether!

The hospital closed in 1976.

Within the Fordham area, we had our own zoo, the famed Bronx Zoo. Entrance to the zoo on Monday and Thursday cost twenty-five cents for adults and fifteen cents for children under twelve years of age. The other days and holidays were free. During the summer, when we were inclined to visit the zoo, many of the nonpoisonous snakes were removed from the Reptile House to a moat-encircled lawn nearby. The New York Zoological Society was known to treat the inmates of the zoo with great care, placing ailing ones in a special hospital, under the care of expert veterinarians. Treatments ranged from extracting hippopotamus molars to curing bronchitis in monkeys.

Our visits, or, rather, our errands that took us to the Fordham Road area were limited to shopping at Alexander's or Roger's Department Store or in Little Italy or visiting grandaunt Gabriella. Much like other immigrant households at that time, our life revolved within a contained environment. Families proceeded warily to understand and adjust to the customs of the New World, not venturing beyond secure daily household or work routines and shopping at familiar neighborhood stores or when possible, at ethnic stores.

Once a year, Papa would take Mama, Natalia, and me to

Manhattan—a special occasion in our lives. We would be dressed in the fine new suits he crafted for us every Easter. Our destination was an upscale clothing store on Fifth Avenue where he worked, and we would greet his boss, who would admire our suits. Despite living in America for ten years before my birth and comporting himself with ease in Manhattan, for dinner, we would always go to the same Italian restaurant owned by a *paesano*—a fellow countryman—and once, as an entertainment, watched a movie of the opera *Il Trovatore*. Papa's attachment was still to the familiarity and comfort he felt within the milieu of his native land. Perhaps this wariness is true of immigrants at all times, but today, computer information affords the current immigrant some idea of America and its customs and may ease assimilation to the New World.

Characteristically, keeping within the confines of the culturally familiar world, we never ventured to the famous Yankee Stadium even though it was within the Fordham Road area. Perhaps we were unaware of how accessible it was. The only sport Mama and Papa were cognizant of was soccer, which Mama's two brothers played in Italy. Nor did we venture further than Alexandra's Department Store to visit one of the most historic sites in the area: Poe Cottage. We did not even know of its existence. Poe's child wife, Virginia, was dying from tuberculosis, and in 1846, Poe, Virginia, and Virginia's mother, Maria Clemm, moved to the Bronx hoping the reputed country air would alleviate Virginia's condition. Having already written "The Raven," Poe was famous at the time, but poverty-stricken. Maria Clemm would scour the neighboring fields for edible herbs to feed the three of them, but Virginia died. Poe was shattered but managed to write some of his descriptive poems in the cottage, such as "Eureka," his requiem for "Virginia," Annabel Lee," and "Ulalume." He left the cottage for Richmond, in 1849.

One of the most enduring memories from the Fordham Road

area was Loew's Paradise Theatre. I will forever recall the majestic, fairy-tale like building that, which in my fanciful child's imagination, surged forth out of Aladdin's lamp. During the World War II years, a family friend, Mrs. Sento, who had an automobile, took Mama, Natalia, and me to the Theatre. Mrs. Sento was hardly interested in the featured movie, the war film, *Assignment in Brittany,* a film I did not forget, horrified by the scenes of torture, but rather wanted us to see this fabulous palace. The décor of the lavishly furnished Paradise was based on the theme of the Italian Baroque era. Among the surround of classic busts and statues were replicas of Michelangelo's *Day* and *Night,* guarding the tomb of the Medici. The theater also features a grand console organ, the Robert Morton "Wonder Organ." In that era even local theaters were elaborately conceived. The theaters were perhaps the most elaborate buildings some children of the era would ever enter. They also provided a dreamy escape for the hard-pressed populace during the Depression era.

After the movie, Mrs. Sento treated us to a nearby Schrafft's, a chain restaurant, which had started as a candy manufacturer. Schrafft's chocolates were a popular gift during those times. As we sat at the fountain service counter, Natalia and I, eating one of the current popular ice cream sundaes, I looked around and experienced a sense of awe and felt somewhat uncomfortable. In feeling, this restaurant was not like Papa's *paesano's* restaurant we went to once a year. To me, that restaurant, with its Southern Italian cuisine and reverberations of conversations in Italian around the room, felt familiar and friendly. I glanced at Mama and Mrs. Sento to see if they had the same sensations, but they were busily chatting away in Italian.

I could not have understood then that Schrafft'a sought to emulate the gentility of the upper class and created refined settings as well as menus reproducing dishes favored by the upper class. I was still contained within the milieu of my ethnic household, which was holding on to its old-world customs while making continual efforts to secure a solid foothold in the New World, let alone striving to attain upper class gentility.

Aside from the immigrants' wariness of treading new grounds, in the absence of automobiles, society at large lived within contained boundaries. But, as the decades rushed towards the twenty-first century, automobiles, jet planes, and lightweight clothes and luggage, transformed America into a mobile society. In 1955, when Mama, Natalia, and I embarked on our first trip to Italy, at that time, aboard an Italian transatlantic ocean liner, we packed our best outfits. I brought one of Anton's fine suits and my expensive black pumps, for traveling by ship, unlike by plane, held a sense of ceremony.

With an expanded awareness of changes in our neighborhood and with greater economic prosperity, families started to go out for dinner. With this change in mores, modest restaurants, and fast-food restaurants, such as White Castle on Fordham Road, began to buy plots on neighborhood streets and put up their signs.

Until decades later in America, cafés, which were long established in Europe, including France and Italy, were no part of our lives. There was no concept of establishing a neighborhood café to provide a pleasant pastime. The capitalistic thrust of America was toward commercialism and enterprising entrepreneurship. The New World had no time for sitting and enjoying a cup of coffee in the easy atmosphere of a café, removed from the cares and worries of home. It had no time to be inspired to write a poem or two or to musingly transport oneself to a café in Paris, where Hemingway, sipping absinthe, might be fostering ideas for a projected novel.

Perhaps the closest resemblance to café leisure time was the soda fountain, where older adolescents and adults socialized. However, soda fountains, along with the popular banana split sundae, were no part of the customs of the families in our neighborhood. Ice cream parlors were generally favored by the elite. If we did eat ice cream, it was only in summer, for the concept of freezing food had not yet entered households. We had a gas refrigerator, and some neighbors still had iceboxes, the ice provided by the iceman, lifting the large chunks with ice thongs. Our source of summer ice cream was the jingling "Bungalow Bar," making its rounds in our neighborhood, selling ice cream for ten cents. If a family had three children, perhaps thirty cents daily on those summer nights was a burden, for in the Depression days, people were hard-pressed financially.

In some houses, meals were put together frugally. Breakfast might simply be bread soaked in milk, and dinners were economical dishes using offal, such as scrapple or the Italian soffritto. For some, a main dish may have consisted of pane cotto, cooked stale bread seasoned with olive oil. In the house of one of my American friends, dinner was often just fried baloney.

We were fortunate, due to Papa's superior tailoring skills, and we continued to eat healthy traditional Italian fare. Even in a slow season in the tailoring trade, Papa continued working, making suits for private customers in his small shop in our apartment adjacent to the back stairs. Added to the generation's financial woes, particularly for emigrants from Europe, was the outbreak of war in Europe, in 1939. Papa and Mama wondered if they would ever cross the Atlantic Ocean again to visit family.

It was thanks to Papa's efforts and his steady income that Mama's and my immigration to America went smoothly. Perhaps other immigrants had relatives in America who also paved the way for them, but for many, early life in the New World was filled with hardship and anguish. Such was the first year of my grandaunt Gabriella.

My grandaunt Gabriella lived on Hoffman Street, in the Fordham Road Area, not too far from the Little Italy neighborhood. I remember her as a kind and sweet relative who was always at our Christmas table. Her gifts to Natalia and me were always a pair of heavy wool ski pants--loose pants drawn in at the ankles—or heavy wool zippered leggings. She was very close to Mama, her beloved niece.

Gabriella was my maternal grandmother's sister and the most beautiful of the four sisters. She had chestnut hair and the straight nose and arched lips of the Grecian profile. She was destined, speculated her neighbors in Montevetuso, to lead a privileged life, by which they meant saved from that Southern Italian curse, *miseria*. To lead a better life, materially, however, did not mean to enjoy a happier life.

Gabriella was in love with Corrado, a cabinetmaker, who was working in *l'America,* or New York City, which to many Italians then was America. She could not wait until his return in one year, for they were to be betrothed. Marriageable men were becoming fewer and fewer, and when Corrado did return, another family snatched him for its daughter. Brokenhearted, Gabriella vowed never to marry.

Shortly after, Gabriella was courted by another suitor, Agostino. Agostino had immigrated to America and worked as a skilled mechanic on New York City's trolley cars. Returning to Montevetuso to find an Italian wife, he was introduced to Gabriella, who, however, remained distant. Besides not feeling the love for him she still felt for Corrado, she knew marriage to Agostino meant emigration to America.

Agostino returned to America, but several years later, after World War I, he tried his luck again with the beautiful Gabriella, who, meanwhile, had a change of heart, or more accurately, a change of mind, for family and friends awakened her to dreary prospects, even for such a beautiful woman as she.

"Take a sober look at how unmarried women spend their lives," her mother, Vittoria, warned her. "You will become a sour spinster or the never fulfilled aunt doting on all your nieces and nephews, and looking back on your life, you will wish you had had a family of your own."

Vittoria's manner became severe, perhaps because Gabriella was already in her mid-twenties. "If you continue being distraught over this lost love, while Corrado is happily married, apparently forgetting you, you might as well join your lovelorn cousin Ada and enter a convent." Upset, she lapsed into silence, before adding, "And end your days there."

If halfheartedly, Gabriella consented to marry Agostino and immigrated to America with him in 1919. Although Agostino had been in America for several years before marrying Augusta, as a single man, he had lived simply and had not managed to pave the way smoothly for his new bride. Gabriella's first experience in America would remain in her mind as a nightmarish experience.

The couple lived in a cold, cramped apartment in a tenement in Lower Manhattan.

All the families on one floor used the one bathroom on the floor. Gabriella was appalled, no, horrified, by the life she perceived that she would be living in the New World, confined to these cold small rooms in this dismal tenement, sitting on a toilet everyone on that floor shared, walking up and down the dark dingy staircase with packages of grocery and sometimes touched with nausea by the smell of boiled cabbage. Was this the grand *l'America* that caused all that emigration stir and bustle in Montevetuso? True, in Montevetuso, in her beige tuff house, there was no bathroom. The family had flower-decorated chamber pots, which were a chore to deal with, but at least the pots were used by family members, not strangers. Besides, here, in the tenement, the toilet was often clogged or the flushing handle did not work. She dreaded the stench when she opened the bathroom door.

Besides the appalling toilet conditions and the dreariness of everyday living, as if in a hole, she was alarmed by rumors that families in the tenement were contracting dreadful diseases. And where, in the New World, was the sun—that blazing heartwarming sun of Italy? No sunlight entered any of the two windows in her apartment, obscured by the narrow street lined with tenements on both sides. In Italy, oh, sunny Italy! The brilliant Mediterranean sun bathed everyone, rich and poor. It shone down on the pots of basil on balconies, on flat roofs—her flat roof, where she dried tomatoes and figs or strung clothes on a line, the whites bleached by those brilliant rays. Thankfully, her stay in such appalling conditions was less than a year, and they moved to the Bronx.

Her apartment on Hoffman Street, which included a bathroom, was clean and roomier, and Gabriella could carry out her everyday chores and shopping more cheerfully and better adjusted. Yet, her longing for Italy and to be with her family, if alleviated by her improved living conditions and more positive attitudes toward life in the New World, never left her. She could not shake off an oppressive feeling of being claustrophobically enclosed in apartments, a feeling synonymous to her with America. She would be well content to return to live in her whitewashed ancestral house on a labyrinthine street behind the cathedral, whose campanile was always under her eye. In the evenings, she looked out her window at the concrete sidewalks below and the gray paved street and nostalgically recalled the evening passeggiata with her girlfriends. It was a simple pleasure, she reflected; it was a simpler life, but there was a place in it for festivity. Her letters to her mother were filled with longing to return to Montevetuso.

She continued to be so homesick and unhappy that Agostino managed to save enough money to send her to Montevetuso more than once, and each time, she returned to America reluctantly. Eventually, she gave birth to a daughter and a son, which put an end to voyages to Montevetuso and fantasies of returning there to live. For her children, Americans with undreamed-of opportunities and for her solidly employed husband, Montevetuso would be a desert, a disaster.

One of the happiest events for Gabriella occurred in the last decade of her life when her niece—Mama and I—immigrated to America. It was as if a piece of Montevetuso, of that now ever-fugitive hill city beneath the dazzling sun of Italy, were transported into her ever-nostalgic life and cast a solacing meridional light across her apartment and on the concrete sidewalks and gray paved street outside. Gabriella and her family visited us frequently. Traveling on the Webster Avenue trolley and then a bus, they carried shopping bags filled with Italian cheeses, cold cuts, imported groceries, and fruit from the markets in Little Italy. (Gabriella's husband, Agostino, was the very same relative who on that unforgettable Christmas Eve could not accommodate Mama by killing the eel.)

In 1940, Gabriella died of a stroke at fifty years old. She would never again make her way up the mountain by horse and carriage, bus, or car, to return to Montevetuso. My grandaunt Gabriella's visits were among the sweetest memories I have of my years on Eastville Avenue.

13

Schooldays

WE LIVED in the furthest outskirts of our school district. In our years at the combined elementary-junior high school, there were no school buses, and our parents did not have automobiles to drive us to school. Our daily walk to school, with our friends, filled with chatter and the woodsy Bronx scenes, took on a character of its own. For some children, the walk constituted the best part of the school day.

Our school attire typically consisted of skirts and blouses or dresses for girls, and shirts and ties for boys, often with corduroy pants. Even as the weather warmed in late spring and summer, we continued to wear laced oxford shoes or older girls, the later current fashion of penny loafers. At that time the prevailing belief was that laced leather shoes, oxfords, helped develop strong feet and healthy walking practices, though for Sunday dress, we wore white Mary Jane shoes. Families often had a baby's first lace-up shoes bronzed as a keepsake.

For our long walk to school, some of us, particularly the girls, carried leather schoolbags to hold schoolbooks, pencil kits, and as we grew older, the much-coveted Waterman fountain pen, though in school, we were still issued the straight pen, with replaceable metal pen points, which we dipped into our ink wells. When not using a schoolbag, girls held books at chest level, boys, with arms straight down, books in hand. One boy in the entire school (perhaps from a German immigrant family) carried his books and perhaps his lunch and other articles in a knapsack. Having no knowledge of such carriers or their name, we thought it very strange to have this large sack supported on one's back.

During the winter months, young children wore woolen ski pants or leggings, which had to be removed in school, and older girls wore long cotton stockings. Rainy days found us all in rubber, from long hooded raincoats to high, clumsy galoshes with buckles, though in 1942, with the rubber shortage during the war, rainy days found us in synthetic rubber.

Now, decades later, perceived through the perhaps romanticized or inventive retention of memory, our daily walk to school has about it a storybook character. Setting off from our houses, we walked toward the heavily wooded acres, beyond where our block ended. There, on our right side, where the woods began, was the deeply recessed pond (which froze in winters not yet afflicted by climate change) where we ice-skated, girls with white ice skates, boys, with black ones. Several girls more skillful than I sought to imitate the virtuosic ice-skating stance of Sonja Henie, the famous Norwegian figure skater and film star we saw in the movies. Sonja Henie would stand on one leg, bend her entire body at an angle, and spread her arms straight out. As far as I can recall, the girls could just about manage to stand on one leg. In spring, from that same swampy area, we picked pussy willows and in late summer, the boys picked cattails, which we called punks, and which they would light with a match, presumably to repel mosquitoes, but more entertainingly, to threaten the girls with the smoldering heads.

We continued our walk, now reaching the trestle. So rural was the northeastern part of the Bronx that, at that time, a two-shuttle car we called the dinkey, starting at Dyre Avenue, took passengers, including Papa, on a workday, to the 180 Street Station where passengers transferred to the regular trains bound for Manhattan. At times as we approached the trestle, we heard the dinkey's clickety-clack before we saw it. We would wait until it reached the part of the trestle right before us, and then we would wave and wave. In warm weather, the passengers would stand on an open deck at the back of the shuttle and wave to us.

On we walked, and taking a shortcut, descended a path leading into another forested area. Our path ran along a narrow stream of water bound on either side by a low brick wall. Perhaps that manmade wall in the woods had a function pertaining to water control, but we children saw it as a source of recreation and would try to walk on the wall, balancing ourselves. The crowning glory of the entrance to that path was the honey locust tree blooming in spring with white heavily scented flowers. One year, I picked some of the flowers and put them in a vase in our parlor. The fragrance was so overwhelming as I practiced the piano that I had to move the vase to the kitchen.

Emerging from the woods, we came upon a white stucco house where a white goat was tethered to a nearby tree. We were fascinated by the goat's goatee and named it Billy Goat Gruff, after the fairy tale, "Three Billy Goats Gruff." In the same yard stood a fig tree, wrapped like a mummy in winter, with an inverted bucket on its head. Most likely, an Italian family lived here, nostalgic for the figs of Italy and the goats, which were source of milk.

Finally, we reached the school and the chain link fence setting off the playground area, which was empty of the colorful play and sport apparatuses highlighting today's school playgrounds. We walked this fairy tale walk four times a day, despite Eastville Avenue being at the last reaches of the school district, for we did not want to bring a brown bag lunch to eat in school. We went home for lunch.

In my Italian household, meals meant cooked foods or antipasto style. Sandwiches were put together only for an outing, such as our occasional trips to Orchard Beach, or for high school years, when home lunches were no longer possible. On a Monday, Mama might have made a dish of cornmeal with the tomato sauce left over from Sunday. She often made pastina, particularly if there was soup leftover from every Monday's chicken soup for dinner. Sometimes she made pastina with butter choosing our favorite shapes of little stars or alphabet letters. Often, a small dessert glass filled with chocolate pudding ended lunch, but soon after, its sweet taste turned fishy, as Mama spooned us our daily tablespoon of cod liver oil. Then, off we went, Natalia and I and the children on the block, to walk our storybook journey for the third time in a day to the afternoon school session, beginning at one.

One year, on the last day of school, a rainy day greeted us as we set out on our customary long walk to school, clad in our raincoats and galoshes. At the end of the school day, we bade our classmates goodbye, for we would not see them again until September, when we returned in spiffy new clothes and new marbled black and white hard-or-soft-covered homework books, as we called them.

I can't quite recall how the confusion took place, but on that last rainy day, I accidentally wore my classmate Francis's galoshes home. We had both entered the classroom simultaneously and placed our galoshes close together. Probably, he had picked up mine and left for home. I do not know if mine fit him, but his were a little large for me. Francis, a son of the local Italian baker, was a thin, pale, and quiet small-statured boy, unobtrusive, in fact, hardly noticeable in the class. Knowing that I would not see him again until September, I placed his galoshes in our closet, and seeing them now and then, imagined them to feel mournful, sadly abandoned. Somehow, the opening of the galoshes, ready for Francis to slip his shoed feet into each one seemed like a mouth opening, calling him.

Occasionally, carrying out errands for Mama, I would skip and hop through the shortcut between the two woods, one with the wondrous towering tulip tree, to go to his father's bread bakery. There, I would buy a pound of pizza dough for ten cents or a favorite crusty loaf, which among other Baroque shapes of loaves, rose high, like a bishop's miter, and finished off in four points. Curiously, I made no connection between Francis and the bakery, where I might have returned his galoshes and asked for mine.

In the middle of that summer, an article in the local paper, the freely-delivered *Home News,* or later called, *The Bronx Home News,* identifying the family, reported that the Italian baker's wife, Francis's mother, turned on the oven and gassed herself and her six children. Francis's mournful galoshes remained in a closet in our house, now truly sadly abandoned and, it seemed to me, weeping.

The tragedy unfolded considerably over half a century ago, and I cannot recall the ultimate fate of Francis's galoshes. Sadly, he was no longer with us as our class continued on toward graduation. Yet, in a way he was, because in the minds of his classmates, he attained a certain immortality, registered right here, in my recollections — a fate he could have hardly attained without that sad, dismaying death.

Much like Proust's madeleines in his *Remembrance of Things Past,* Francis's and my galoshes, retained in the archives of memory, find their way into literature. In my memory, within the hallway clothing closet of our first-floor apartment on Eastville Avenue, sit Francis's galoshes, forever weeping.

My favorite part of school, in the 1930s and 1940s, was Assembly Day. Assembly Day took place twice a week, on Mondays and Thursdays. We were required to dress up for the occasion: girls wore white blouses, and boys, who always wore ties, added white shirts to their attire. Assembly took place in the modest-sized auditorium, in which the stage was a several-foot long rectangular wooden platform, just elevated enough and wide enough to do what a stage does: raise given moments in life above the floor level to a higher one, adding a bit of wing and soar to words and gesture or taking off outright in song.

Assembly, marshalling a range of middle and upper grades, served to develop a sense of unity in the school student body. Although mostly dedicated to singing community and folk songs, occasionally teachers planned a different activity. When we marched into the auditorium and saw a camera with a giant reel and a large white screen up front, we knew we would see a movie. Although all of us were eager to watch the movie, for some of the children of that era, who perhaps did not even have a radio in the house and were too poor to attend a movie, which cost twenty-five cents, watching movies at assembly was a favorite activity.

On one occasion, the teacher asked the student body if anyone played the piano and would like to perform for the assembly. I, ten years old, small for my age, walked to the Krakauer parlor grand, and performed "Rustle of Spring," by Christian Sinding, astounding the assembly and teachers who henceforth looked upon me somewhat as a prodigy and had me play the piece for the subsequent graduation ceremony. When students saw me outside school, they nicknamed me, "Rustle of Spring."

On the wall of the auditorium were large gold-framed paintings of Sir Lawrence's *Pinkie,* and Thomas Gainsborough's, *The Blue Boy.* The paintings gave life to that auditorium, for the students looked forward to seeing these two young children awaiting them on assembly days. The painted children brought a vestigial sense of beauty into the lives of the students, most of whom were from families of modest income. *Blue Boy* and *Pinkie* might well have been their first inkling of the world of art. None of us knew then that Pinkie, who was about eleven years old when the painting was completed, died one year later. Nor did we know that the famous poet Elizabeth Barrett Browning was her niece.

Many years later, visiting my elementary school, I walked into the auditorium and stopped short, exclaiming, "Oh!" The children, Pinkie and Blue Boy, were gone! Hastening to the school office I asked, "Where are the paintings?" They had been removed into the principal's office for fear they would be stolen! Gone, yes, from that wall, but not for those of us who have not yet vanished. The two children are still on that wall, waiting for us on assembly days, Monday and Thursday.

As vivid to me today as *Pinkie* and *Blue Boy*, is the tall, somewhat gaunt, gray-haired music teacher Miss Duane. She introduced us to a wide range of community songs, which also included folk songs, and who taught the required music-listening class to upper-grade students. For that music hour, we would sit in the classroom looking at the RCA Victor gramophone as she dropped the needle on the 78 rpm records, identifying the light classical music she had chosen for us to listen to, such as Percy Granger's "Country Gardens"; Edvard Grieg's "In the Hall of the Mountain King," from *Peer Gynt;* Tchaikovsky's "Andante Cantabile," which Tchaikovsky arranged from his String Quartet no. 1; and "To a Wild Rose," by Edward MacDowell. She told us that Edward MacDowell and his pianist wife founded the MacDowell Colony, an artists' colony, in New Hampshire. We listened to our teacher attentively, but many of the students, including me, did not know where New Hampshire was. Miss Duane also taught the Glee Club.

Standing tall at the front of the auditorium, passionately dedicated Miss Duane lead us through our sizeable repertoire, with which we, also standing, filled assembly hour. One of our favorite songs was, "Billy Boy," in which "charming Billy" is in search of a wife, a woman, who is "the joy of his life." In stanza after stanza, Billy is asked about the woman's household skills and upstanding character (church attendance), in all of which, as Billy asserts, she is outstanding. Every stanza ends with the refrain that she is too young to leave her mother. When asked, "How old may she be, / Billy Boy, Billy Boy?" Billy Boy replies with a long series of numbers, adding up to age eighty-two, concluding, "But she's a young thing / And cannot leave her mother."

Another of our favorite songs was, "My Grandfather's Clock," about the clock that was taller than the old man himself, weighed not a pennyweight more, and stood ninety years on the floor. The clock was bought on the day the old man was born and was his pride and treasure. Particularly gleeful to sing was the line, "Tick, tock, tick, tock," in the chorus, but the children then changed their glee to drama, as they emphatically sang the chorus's last two lines: "But it stopped, short, never to go again / When the old man died." Of course, considering that a grandfather's clock must be wound daily or weekly, it is understandable that the clock stopped when the old man died, but according to our interpretation, when the grandfather died, the clock died, for it had no more desire to live.

Among the songs we learned were the melancholy "Flow Gently, Sweet Afton," the British World War I song, "It's a Long, Long Road to Tipperary, "Loch Lomond," "Believe Me If All Those Endearing Young Charms," "The Lost Chord," the hymn, "Abide with Me, "and an English translation of "Panis Angelicus," but perhaps the most hauntingly beautiful song was, "The Linden Tree," which relates that beneath an old stone fountain, stands a linden tree, which brought glad dreams to the singer.

We did not know that Schubert composed, "The Linden Tree" as well as "Who is Sylvia?" which Miss Duane also taught us. "The Linden Tree," was excerpted from Schubert's *Die Winterreise, The Winter Journey,* which Schubert wrote when he was dying, and which explains the overwhelming sadness, the sheer pathos, of the song. We remained unaware that Afton was in

Scotland or that Tipperary was in Ireland and that it was a famous marching song in World War I. We did not know that loch in Scottish means lake and that Lake Lomond was also in Scotland.

Teaching a good-sized student body, a large repertoire of community and folk songs, Miss Duane had a monumental task to perform, within the limits of the Monday and Thursday hour for Assembly. Explanations and the history of musical pieces were better served in her music listening class. These classic songs, passed on from generation to generation, stayed with us for the rest of our lives.

14

From the Insular Block to the Wide World

ALTHOUGH OUR DAILY lives and play were more or less confined within the limits of the city block, we had the means to seek diversions and be lifted out of it in three different ways, one of which did not even call for us to step out of our houses. All that was required was a fairly common household apparatus, a viewless medium called a radio. We were a generation that could sit still for an hour or more without moving visual scenes engaging our attention.

On Sunday afternoons, at 5:30, Natalia and I would sit close to our radios and listen to "The Shadow," awaiting the spooky opening music auguring a good spellbinding mystery for the next half hour (the music was an excerpt from Saint-Saëns's *Omphale's Spinning Wheel*). As the mystery unfolded, we were working our imagination to envision the scenes of the story and what The Shadow looked like. To me, he appeared literally as a shadow of a masked face on a wall, and, of course, Margo Lane was as beautiful as a movie star, for there were not many other sources of what was currently considered beautiful that we could refer to other than the movies. Every boy on the block would try to mimic The Shadow's eerie filtered voice, sometimes that of Orson Wells, and his sardonic laugh: *Who knows what evil lurks in the hearts of men. The Shadow knows.* The end of the program always left us with the dire warning that, "Crime does not pay."

The Shadow, who led a double life, inspired the creation of Superman, Batman, and Captain Marvel. He was a vestige of the nineteenth century, which was intrigued by the mysterious in the human mind, the demonic; the mind motivated by a spiritual force or genius, reaching toward transcendence, toward, perhaps, occult knowledge. The Shadow could have easily been a character out of a tale by E.T.A. Hoffman, a fascinating Mephistophelian figure.

On Saturday morning at 11:30, we listened to "Let's Pretend," a program that dramatized fairy tales. Images of television would probably not have achieved the explosive dazzle brilliantly flashing in my mind as I listened to "The Snow Queen." I envisioned the snow queen's palace of driven snow, with more than a hundred frozen halls lit by the Northern Lights and the snow queen herself, dressed in a luminous snow-gossamer gown laced with frost and sparkling with crystal sequins.

"Inner Sanctum," with occasional appearances by Boris Karloff as guest star, appealed to children's fascination, if tinged with fright, with ghosts or macabre stories. The program opened with a heavy, squeaking door that slowly and ominously gave way to the inner sanctum and to who knew what horror in that episode. In my child's mind, the inner sanctum was like a dungeon with a skull or two lying about. At the end of the horror, the door to the inner sanctum slowly and heavily squeaked closed.

In accordance with the time, the 1940s, the horror stories had more in common with the style of Edgar Allen Poe than the violent, sexually perverse, and pathological aberrations often found in today's horror stories. The horror of former times still clung to literary precepts, old-fashioned storytelling, to fascinate and entertain, like Mary Shelly's *Frankenstein*.

Movies were the second form of diversion that drew us away from our city block. On Saturday afternoons, Natalia, Helina, and I, sometimes accompanied by our friends, Claudette, Judy, and Lila, would walk up the block, cross Gun Hill Road, and venture down long blocks to Boston Road, on which were two movie houses, a Loew's and a Melba, named after Dame Nellie Melba (as was Melba toast), a popular Australian opera star. We were walking toward what we knew as the "Hillside Homes," but we had no idea what they looked like or that they were built in the northeastern Bronx in 1934-35 and were one of first middle-class subsidized homes in the country.

Part of our eagerness to see the scheduled movie was the enchantment of stepping inside the movie theater, which transported us into an Arabian Nights setting. Although not as lavish as the fabulous Loew's Paradise Theatre, our local Loew's theater, on Boston Road, had a bijou—a jewellike outdoor ticket booth. The lush interior with its tones of red and gold, plush carpeting, soft recessed lights, exotic décor (probably Art Deco motifs), and deep red velvet seats swept us completely off the city block into the world of Aladdin and his magic lamp. Sometimes, Helina's aunt joined us, and she would take us to "The Ladies' Powder Room." We would descend a staircase into a lush outer lounge with cushioned chairs and lustrous mirrors before entering the restroom.

My father strictly supervised the movies Natalia and I could see, that is, the main film, the *A* film, though standard at that time was a double bill, which included the *B* film, plus newsreels and sometimes a cartoon. Musicals were permitted and children's films, such as *The Wizard of Oz*, in the new spectacular mode of Technicolor. Vying with the wonder of *The Wizard of Oz* was *Fantasia*, which bewitched us, particularly the thumpa, thumpa, thumpathumpathump of the symphonic poem, *The Sorcerer's Apprentice*, as the consternated Mickey Mouse desperately tries to stop the relentless momentum of the water-fetching broom.

In addition to musicals, Papa permitted adventure movies, particularly those featuring the swashbuckling Errol Flynn. Among the musicals, *Knickerbocker Holiday* (1944), with Nelson Eddy, remains foremost in my mind, for it featured Kurt Weill's classic heart-stirring "September Song," and the slow, sadly contemplative melody of the chorus: "Oh, the days whittle by to a precious few / September, November."

Papa also permitted biographical movies, and we saw movies featuring the lives of Gershwin; Marie Antoinette; Madame Curie; Tchaikovsky, 1948, *Song of My Heart;* and Chopin, 1945, *A Song to Remember.* We took these films seriously, as authentic representations of the various lives, which, of course, was not so. In a movie about Tchaikovsky, I recall a scene in which the camera fixed dramatically upon a glass of water, the lethal liquid, that would cause Tchaikovsky to contract cholera, which killed him—a simplistic, quasi naïve movie image but powerful in its impact upon us as children. (Today, Tchaikovsky's death by cholera has been questioned, as other theories emerged.)

Despite the romanticized biographies, for us, these films were instructive and influential. While I was inspired by musical biographies, many schoolgirls were influenced by Hollywood's glamorous portrayal of secretaries and opted to take the commercial course in high school. We learned of current celebrated artists we would never see: ballerina Vera Zorina; opera singer Risë Stevens; pianists Oscar Levant and José Iturbi, the Spanish pianist who introduced into the current piano repertoire Manuel de Falla's "Ritual Dance of Fire" (arranged for piano), Debussy's "Clair de Lune," and Chopin's "Heroic" Polonaise, in A-flat major, piano pieces I immediately learned.

Several years later, I would see celebrated pianists—Arthur

Rubenstein, Eugene Istomin--for twenty-five cents, at the Lewisohn Stadium, the amphitheater on the campus of the City College of New York. Bravura performances of piano concertos would resound through the New York City surround, if now and then drowned out by the drone of an airplane overhead.

After the movies, we walked home dreamily, hardly aware of turning left off Boston Road, walking through the long blocks, crossing Gun Hill Road and onto our block. Saturday, movie day, was a day of great anticipation that transported us to different places, making us aware of other people, the dramatis personae, expanding the limited perceptions and square feet of our lives on one block, in the Bronx of long ago.

The third way of emerging out of the insularity of the block was perhaps the greatest in helping to develop our character and awakening us to perceive the containment of our life on our cozy city block and the need to emerge from its maternal embrace. The third way opened our eyes wide to the diversity of ways of living and of human destinies, out there through the continents and seas of the earth.

"There is no Frigate like a Book," wrote Emily Dickinson, "To take us Lands away." Our frigate was a large truck. Learning of this truck, perhaps through our local *Bronx Home News* or through school, Natalia, Helina, and I made our way past the local stores on Gun Hill Road and shortly beyond, to Eastchester Road. The side of the truck read The New York Public Library. We call it the traveling library (not a bookmobile). Upon first stepping inside and seeing the two walls solidly lined with differently colored hardback books, we were struck with wonder. This became our *Secret Garden*, like Mary's, in Francis Hodgson Burnett's *The Secret Garden*.

This enchanted realm existed amidst the backdrop of ordinary life: trucks transporting produce along Eastchester and Gun Hill Roads, shoppers clutching bags filled with delicatessen goods, round loaves of Italian bread, or newly mended shoes, and the clatter, clatter, clatter of the dinkey approaching Gun Hill Road Station to pick up, or let out, passengers.

For our immigrant parents, this incredible municipal action of conveying books to their children was ... was America! It held the same significance as the Statue of Liberty they, and Mama, holding me in her arms, breathlessly awaited to cast their eyes upon as their transatlantic liner sailed into New York Harbor.

Natalia and I possessed a small collection of children's hardcover books, including *Pinocchio, Oliver Twist, The Prince and the Pauper, Hans Brinker or the Silver Skates,* and one or two of Johanna Spyri's Heidi books, as translated from German. Occasionally, the books had colored illustrations, which aided us as we worked our imagination to evoke images of characters in books, as, for example, Captain Nemo in *Twenty Thousand Leagues under the Sea.* We went on to read other Jules Verne's books, such as, *Around the World in Eighty Days,* and *The Mysterious Island,* not aware then that we were reading translations from the French.

Frequenting this marvelous library on its scheduled day of the week, we made our way through the children's book, starting with *The Five Little Peppers and How They Grew,* and the tearful Elsie Dinsmore melodramas. We moved onto books by Louis May Alcott and Frances Hodgson Burnett's. Drawn into mysteries, I discovered the Nancy Drew series, but was spellbound when I stumbled upon Augusta Huiell Seaman mysteries, of which she wrote more than forty and of which the library had a generous collection. To this day, the title, *The Sapphire Signet,"* summons up a period of feverish reading, as I checked out every single Seaman book in the library.

I exhausted the Sue Barton nurse, series, the first career novels for adolescence. I then traveled to the West and books by Zane Grey, a favorite being *Riders of the Purple Sage,* subsequently veering to the East, following the adventures of Natty Bumpo in James Fennimore Cooper's *Leatherstocking Tales*. Popular, then, too, was *Robinson Crusoe* and Sir Walter Scott's *Ivanhoe*.

We were thrilled by Rafael Sabatini's swashbuckling novels, particularly *Scaramouche*, and in the same swashbuckling vein, we read Baroness Emmuska Orczy's popular novel, *The Scarlet Pimpernel*. We landed up in France, reading the novels of Alexandre Dumas père, including *Les Misérable,* recalling our evenings listening to Papa, near mesmerized by his-up-and-down moving sewing hand.

Books introduced us to words we had never heard in our ethnic household: cupboard, dresser, wardrobe, and specific descriptive words for general terms as used in my household: bonnet, instead of hat; armchair, instead of chair; saucepan or kettle, instead of pot; blanket, instead of cover.

It was inevitable. We were being weaned away from our block. The street was widening. We felt the urge to thrust ahead, there, onto that horizon far beyond Gun Hill Road, even beyond the Hillside Homes. We were becoming blushingly conscious of our "Bronxese" and sought to emulate speech as we heard it spoken by our teachers, radio announcers, and movie actors, though in unguarded moments we lapsed back into Bronxese, so strong is the impress of a child's first learning of a language.

The block could no longer contain us, and our insularity began to crumble. In a major push, some of us thrust onward to the British novels, John Galsworthy's *Forsyte Saga,* in which, as in the novels of Edith Wharton, I was introduced to upper middle-class protagonists and patterns of life as foreign from my ethnic background as the Asians Marco Polo visited. I picked up knowledge of foreign specialties and goods: Wedgewood pottery, china, Darjeeling tea (we made tea only as a medicinal beverage, primarily chamomile tea), Irish linen, Belgian lace, Madeira wine, Gobelin tapestries, Aubusson rugs.

The world beyond the city block was incredibly rich, how immensely full of places and objects unknown to us, the children on the block, to Helina, Natalia, and me. I was graduating to a different order of taste from the handsome but baroque décor, that furniture, that wallpaper, of my immigrant household. Yet even beyond décor, the laces, tapestries, and rugs, books introduced to us their literary characters, caught up in passions and sorrows and in dramatic scenes, expanding our perception of life itself, all the possible happenings. Whether consciously or not, we started to fashion our personalities out of bits and pieces of literary characters who had impressed us and imitated turns of phrases we read. We were awakening to larger, deeper emotions than was possible to experience in our sheltered little lives on the city block.

15

Commencement, an Ending and a Beginning

THE STOOPS of our houses served as the bridge between the sheltered indoors and the warm embrace of the neighborhood, releasing our minds into creative hours of sidewalk games, street games, and board games, as we sat in backyards planted with gardens and an occasional fruit tree. The stoop knew we were detaching from our childhood and the block.

The stoop, eight concrete steps leading to the front door, was a record of the passage of my young years into adolescence. I went up and down those steps in leggings, ski pants, oxford shoes, and my Sunday Mary Jane's. Then as a teenager and conscious of fashion, I stepped onto the stairs of my stoop with my loafers and white and brown saddle shoes. Now, auspiciously, on the way to adulthood, my shoes became heeled and wedged, a popular style of the 1940s. With the changes in shoes, heeled and wedged, came the change from my childhood bangs and two tufts of hair pulled back with ribbons to the current style in vogue, the *pageboy*.

Now, from stepping to "A, my name is Anna," "Teddy Bear," and "Rin, Tin, Tin," my friends and I stepped to the glee and jubilance of jitterbug that had America hopping and swinging. We swung through the Lindy Hop (named after Charles Lindbergh), the Charleston, and our version of The Big Apple (a dance craze of 1937), for which Helina wore her Big Apple Skirt, a flared white skirt with a border of red apples.

From the "bobby socks" and brown and white saddle shoes, I moved to silk stockings. Those first moments of putting on silk stockings, sliding the stockings slowly up the leg, ensuring that the seams were straight, a line leading seductively clear up the dress, transforming the leg into a breathless shapeliness created within me a sensation that I was leaving childhood behind. We called our stockings silk stockings, but they were actually made of a new substance called *nylon,* invented in the late 1930s, a mere few years before I donned them.

During World War II, nylon was diverted to military purposes and used to make parachutes, among other war materials. As nylon became scarce, women resorted to rayon stockings. Rayon, made from wood cellulose, became known as "artificial silk" and filled in for the nylon shortage during the war. Some girls and women went so far as to buy leg makeup and painted their legs, including a seam down the back of their leg to mimic the appearance of stockings. It did not matter to me if the stockings I carefully slipped up my legs were from actual silk or nylon or wood. It was the gesture of slipping them on, imbuing me with the feeling that childhood was shedding from me and that now a new Annalisa would be stepping down the stoop onto a block, no longer there cozily and permanently for me. I would gain entrance into that circle of older girls I would watch with childhood curiosity, wondering what secrets they were whispering about. And where were these stockings, neatly folded, placed but in a bureau drawer, it, too, debuting into girlhood, no longer the matter-of-fact receptacle for storing a child's underwear and pajamas.

That drawer emanates a radiant glow as it becomes imbued with new meaning. Glance into it and comprehend there, as well as in family photograph albums, the development from childhood to adolescence. A fragrant soap or sachet assumes a new purpose as it is put in that drawer or to scent undergarments, brassieres, assuming feminine shapes and decorated with enchanting lace. Other personal effects are introduced: hair decorations, perhaps fancy barrettes; Yardley of London's scented flowered paper packages of powdered chamomile shampoo for blond hair; a jar of deodorant; and in a second drawer, a box of Kotex, for me, newly discovered.

Following Mama's custom, I had previously relied on strips of sheets, washed and reused. Having become aware of a magazine called, *Calling all Girls,* through the influence of friends, I bought a copy and learned of the packaged sanitary napkins. Beyond that, simply owning my own private magazine was precious and grownup, and I placed it in that second drawer. My two secret drawers added a new dimension to my life. It was the beginning of a turn toward introspection from a child's innocent openness welcoming the flow of life into its uninhibited gaze. These bodily changes filled me with a hushed awe, but the secret aura surrounding my two drawers might well have been reinforced by our era, an era when intimate apparel, such as brassieres or other underwear, of women or men or adolescents, were considered personal matters and not broached in public. I never even touched upon these subjects with my best friend Helina. Besides, perhaps through temperament as well as the customs of the era, I have always maintained reticence in relation to feminine hygiene and cosmetics. I cannot even say the word *menstruate,* today, without a feeling of diffidence. Not only was this natural biological development a hushed subject, at least within my milieu, but it was also encumbered by social beliefs that in that physical state, activities were to be curtailed.

Swimming, for instance, was to be avoided, perhaps as much for the risk of revealing bulky underwear as for beliefs pertaining to health.

Skipping several years ahead, I recall two particular moments when I had that same feeling of initiation into adulthood. One was the day I inserted my first dime into the subway slot of the Third Avenue El, on my first day of attending college. I felt as if I were drawn into the embrace of the city —the great New York City! I had become an integral part of the subway-riding community, finding my then wicker seat among the men in fedoras and the women, with feathers or flowers or ribbons or netting on their stylish hats, perhaps a few Lilly Daché hats. Above us, in summer, ceiling fans kept us cool, if undoing a hair arrangement. I was unquestionably an adult now, navigating my way alone in the wondrous city.

The other was a magical moment in the cafeteria of college, when I was a senior, sitting down with classmates, all young women, in the all-women college, and drinking a cup of coffee. Coffee! How adult I felt! How, in that cup of coffee, I, now an adult, felt an exhilarating sense of embracing the world, or rather, the great city of New York, the Empire State Building, the Chrysler building, the New York Public Library with the famed two lions on its steps, the Museum of Metropolitan Art, of Modern Art, the Metropolitan Opera House. The exaltations of the grand buildings summoned me, filled with youthful aspiration to compass their heights and grandeur. There was so much I had to do and would do! All this, in a cup of coffee!

Returning to the 1940s, I and my friends from the block were undergoing the transition from adolescence into adulthood. In June 1945 we graduated from our eight-term elementary school. As was traditional, we were to march into the auditorium to the music of Edward Elgar's "Pomp and Circumstance March" no. 1. We were already familiar with the melody of the trio, for Miss

Duane had taught us the lyrics written to it, "Land of Hope and Glory," one of our Assembly songs.

Perhaps some of us were acquainted with the music of "Pomp and Circumstance," while others heard it for the first time. Whatever the future held for us graduates on that day in 1945—whether it meant achieving an illustrious career or faring well in the normal sequence of marriage, children, grandchildren, at that moment of marching to the uplifting melody, we felt a bigness within us, a Commencement. The music touched that potential in everyone to rise to a greater self. At the same time, even as it stirred us to heightened feelings, the melody had a nostalgic cast. We were leaving our childhood days on the city block behind.

Part Four

World War II

16

The Home Front

THE LAST FOUR years of our eight-term elementary school, 1941-1945, were marked by a radical change in our lives. We, the children on the block, continued our seasonal games, listening to the radio shows and attending movies, but, suddenly, a new atmosphere pervaded Eastville Avenue, dissipating our feeling of on-the-block coziness. Eastville Avenue, as with all neighborhoods from the Atlantic to the Pacific Ocean, was thrust from its Avenue confines into the comprehensive turmoil of a nation at war. On December 8, 1941, President Roosevelt declared war on Japan, and by December 11, 1941, President Roosevelt declared war on Germany and Italy. America had entered World War II.

We were already familiar with the word *front*, but during the war, by constantly hearing the word on the radio and in movie newsreels, we learned that the word also meant an armed force's foremost position on a battleground, such as "the Italian Front" or "the French Front." Although here in America, there was no battleground front, the country was nevertheless called a front. Therefore, we were now not only the children of the Great

Depression era but also the children of the American Home Front.

In the earlier years of the war, in the houses on our block, talk of Germany centered on its seemingly invincible strain of warfare, its arrogant, imperialistic triumphant marches into Austria, Poland, and Denmark. We feared that the German army, armed with the Panzer tank divisions, U-boats (submarines, which torpedoed warships and passenger liners), and the Luftwaffle, like the *messerchmitt* bombers deployed in the blitz, might well become a threat on our shores. Cities scheduled air raid drills and we saw long streams of searchlights moving slowly across our night skies, possibly spotting a *messerchmitt* bomber. Weather reports were modified, limited to reporting conditions within a hundred-and-fifty-mile radius, lest sabotaging ongoing military strategy. Wind and barometric pressure were concealed.

Particularly in the first year or so, a wartime hysteria gripped New York City. Mayor LaGuardia warned New Yorkers of the possibility of being bombed by the Germans, as in the London blitz, for we lived along the Atlantic coast. As a further precaution, for us, the Home Front children, Mayor LaGuardia decreed that schoolchildren wear a dog tag, a white plastic disk, an inch or so in diameter attached to a white cotton binding, as used in sewing. The tags were written in cursive and included a serial number. Daily, along with our changing outfits, we wore the dog tag around our neck. Should we have been bombed as we played on the city block or on our adventuresome walk to school, perhaps bombed along with Billy Goat Gruff and the fig tree, the dog tag would identify us.

Periodically, a siren wailed through the city blocks, indicating an air raid drill. During these drills, we peered through our windows and saw the air raid warden patrolling the block, diligently checking every house, ready to shout, "Get those lights out!" He wore a helmet and an armband with the air raid warden insignia: a striped diamond within a circle. He carried a flashlight and a gas mask.

The war left its imprint on popular songs as well. In 1942, crooner Vaughn Monroe sang, "When the lights go on again all over the world," life would be "sweet and simple." Only rain or snow would fall from the skies, ships would sail freely on the seas, and kisses would not mean good-by but "Hello to love." In 1941, in another popular war song (relating to the Blitz in Britain), another crooner assured us that "There'll be bluebirds over / The white cliffs of Dover," in fact, "Tomorrow," and that there will be "love and laughter / And peace ever after." Yet, like the Londoners who took refuge in underground shelters, the bluebirds might have taken refuge in the crevices of Dover. Years would pass, and massive fatalities committed therein, before the bluebirds emerged to fly over Dover.

Like a Puccinian wait-and-see theme—*Un bell dì, vedremo* —these 1941-42 songs proved to be wishful thinking. Air raid drills would continue through the next three years, and the lights of New York City and the Statue of Liberty would remain dimmed.

This war-tinged mentality made us a little more than just children. We were affected by our anxious parents. Some of whom were concerned about their relatives in Europe, and others, about their sons and daughters stationed overseas in the heart of the war arenas. Seeing the Western Union messenger at a neighbor's door, with its fatal purpose, and seeing soldiers walking about in the neighborhood, usually on furloughs, were part of our milieu and thereby our weltanschauung. On the radio or in movie newsreels, we heard the anthems of the armed forces. I particularly liked the jaunty Marine Corps anthem, with its colorful evocation of foreign places: "From the Halls of Montezuma / to the shores of Tripoli." I liked the musical words, Montezuma and Tripoli, but had no idea where they were nor that Montezuma was a person, Emperor Montezuma of Mexico, not a place.

Shopping with our mothers, we saw them carry not only cash but also ration booklets containing stamps used on a points system, and small coins, red and blue plastic tokens worth one point each. On the ration booklets, I read that "this book must not be transferred," violation of which ranged from as high as imprisonment for ten years or a ten thousand dollar fine, or both.

There was a significant effort on our block and generally at large to support the war effort. We were encouraged to buy war bonds, which was a way to help the government finance military spending, and to grow "Victory Gardens," to supplement food supplies, for now great quantities of food were needed to mail by air or ship to our forces overseas.

As children, we actively participated in the war effort by collecting expired newspapers from the neighbors on the block for recycling. We brought our collections to Mr. Strausner, my neighbor to whom I brought Sunday's pasta and meatball dish. Long disabled because of poor lungs, Mr. Strausner lived on health and welfare services as of 1935, when the Social Security Act was passed. Mr. Straussner had formerly been a plumber and had done our plumbing. He was always successful in his repairs but not without considerable swearing in a furious one-way dialogue with an intractable leaky faucet or stopped drainpipe.

Mr. Strausner added our newspapers to his own collection. His daily newspaper was the New York *Journal American*. I remember, atop the first page of the Sunday comics, or as we called them, the funnies, was Puck, in a top hat and frock coat, leaning on a post, and in his other hand, holding a staff with a long curling scroll, reading, "What fools these mortals be!" as in Shakespeare's *Midsummer Night's Dream* (though the Roman philosopher Seneca made the remark much earlier in history). Mr. Strausner stored the newspapers in neatly bundled piles in his basement until eventually taking them to a center for a minimal about of money.

During my childhood, when I conversed with Mrs. Strausner, I noticed she was chewing on something. Over time, I realized that she chewed on a piece of white wax, and sometimes she pressed the white wax along the upper front row of her teeth—her remaining teeth—to camouflage the several missing front teeth. One night, in 1945, sleepless, looking out of the window above the end of my bedstead, I saw an ambulance, and a covered form on a stretcher being brought out of the Strassner house. No, Mrs. Strassner would not be chewing on the white wax or anything anymore, for she died of cancer.

As the war continued, various measures were taken to boost morale. Along with the radio and movie newsreels narrating the progress of the war, were the popular songs, serving almost like an Internet. As the draft continued to summon up more and more men, the Irving Berlin song, "This is the Army Mister Jones," sought to introduce humor into the harsh training for the incoming soldiers. Acknowledging the bravery of our forces was the solemn tune of Ann Seton's song, "Comin' in on a Wing and a Prayer."

17

War on the Bronx Streets and Kilroy

By 1942, the war was infiltrating every aspect of the American populace's lives. Newspapers, movie newsreels, and the music of the times influenced and shaped our thoughts and daily lives, including our street games. The songs and images worked as propaganda, stirring up patriotism and boosting morale.

In our neighborhood, the boys began to create a street language vilifying our enemies. Our era's feel for poetry in play was now directed toward the war, and on our block, I would hear the boy's singsong recitation:

Whistle while you work.
Hitler is a jerk;
Mussolini is a meanie;
But the Japs are worse.

Sometimes they sang the 1943 satirical song, "Der Fuehrer's Face." They might have known only those three words of the song, but they knew what was included in it and gave a good resounding Bronx cheer. Sometimes, even though Russia was an ally, they sang a two-line melody with gobbledygook words and a guileful look: "Oh, shu shungna, oh, shu shungna." Clearly, they did not know what they were saying or where the melody came from.

The melody was the moving, darkly sad opening of "The Volga Boat Song." I recognized the tune because in our house, the radio dial was always set on the New York City classical music station WQXR (owned then by the *New York Times*). At that time, some people might not yet have bought a radio or having bought one, had not yet become habituated to it as an informative and entertaining medium, as, for example, listening to Major League Baseball games. Perhaps neighbors also kept their dial on WQXR, for otherwise, I cannot fathom how the opening strains of the "The Volga Boat Song" made their way onto the city blocks in the rural East Bronx.

During the war, English pianist Dame Myra Hess initiated lunchtime concerts in the National Gallery in London, to boost the morale of the English people, especially during the blitz. Particularly associated with Dame Myra Hess was her transcription of the Bach Chorale, "Jesu, Joy of Man's Desiring." Her concerts were a great success, and whether I became aware of her concerts and transcription during the war or through broadcasts after the war, I always remember her as the wartime pianist and later played her transcription of "Jesu, Joy of Man's Desiring."

From the wartime "street education" of words or snippets of tunes, promulgating through the blocks, all directed toward jeering at the enemy, was a new word, to me: *harikari*. Did I know what it meant? No. Where would I have come across this strange word? Did the children, probably mostly boys, who bandied the word about, know what it meant? *Harikari,* an American English misspelling of *hara-kiri* or harakiri was the term describing the honorable ritual suicide by self-disembowelment practiced by Japanese samurai. The incidence of suicide committed by Japanese soldiers during the war perhaps explains the appearance of that word in the current popular vocabulary. However, it's puzzling how bits of actual happenings, peculiar words, the tone of a discussion in a household, or an item in a newsreel, find their way onto the streets, are picked up by the children, colorfully embroidered by them, and become street talk. It's not unlike the evolving of folk tales, bits of reality melded with fancifulness and sometimes with the grotesque.

The name, Hirohito, was also on the streets, perhaps from many references to him in movie newsreels or newspapers. I recall no particular sentiments or attitudes associated with voicing that name, though it fell easily on the lips. Like Italian, Japanese names usually end in vowels. I am not sure that I learned that he was an emperor, but I might have been astonished, for to me, emperors and kings were in fairy tales, not cognizant at that time that I was born in a kingdom, the Kingdom of Italy!

In the summers, the boys would walk up to the woods at the end of the block and play war games. They would fight the Germans and the "Japs," and they always won. It was part of street talk to refer to the Japanese as "Japs," picked up perhaps from newspaper headlines, hearsay, or from comic books, in which cartoons caricatured the enemy, just as they would a gangster in a regular cartoon series. Another popular activity for the boys, and that also made them feel patriotically active in the war, was to construct American fighter planes with balsa wood and a strong-smelling glue.

Images, such as the government issued posters of Uncle Sam, were popular and effective at boosting morale. While walking to and from school with Helina and Natalia, we would see graffiti on a concrete wall, which read, "Kilroy was here." Kilroy was in many places, for wherever there was an adaptive flat concrete façade,

THE VANISHING GENERATION

Kilroy was there. Who was Kilroy? We wondered, but did not pursue the mystery, since we had no recourse to a source providing the answer. Had we lived decades later, we would have consulted our smartphone, which became an indispensable appurtenance of everyday life, indoors and outdoors. Occasionally, the graffiti was accompanied by a graphic representation of Kilroy, a man with a long nose peering over a wall, which mystified us even more.

I did not learn until years later that Kilroy graffiti was hardly confined to the Bronx but made its way to Europe, following our soldiers wherever they were stationed, amusing them and perhaps confusing enemies, who might have thought that Kilroy was a spy. Kilroy was not only a memento at large of the Second World War but also for us, living our simple lives on the city block. We never found out who Kilroy was.

As children, we read about the war in our editions of *Current Events*, our school's eight-page newspaper. In 1943, the newspaper produced an issue that featured Southern Italy's surrender and the fall of Fascism in the South, news that had great significance for Papa, Mama and me. The newspaper also informed us that the soldiers overseas, coated with mud and in immediate danger of their lives, disliked "sugarcoated propaganda." The public, they feel, should be told more about "the ugly side of war."

Current Events also had a long notable article in 1943 focused on America's treatment of prisoners during the war. It revealed that there were about 140,000 prisoners in America: about 100,000 were German soldiers; the rest were Italian. America received only a certain number of prisoners; the rest were sent to England, Canada, and Australia. Less than a hundred Japanese soldiers were in America, for the Japanese were taught that it is a disgrace to be taken alive, preferring to commit suicide, perhaps in the honored fashion of hara-kiri, and very few gave themselves up.

One of the features of that issue centered on Japan's treatment of American prisoners and alluded to the Geneva Convention, an organization that established standards of international law for humanitarian treatment in war. "Japan never signed the Geneva Convention but promised to abide by its provisions. We do not know whether she is keeping her promise." Perhaps the writer had in mind the Bataan "Death March" of 1942 or the alarming reports about the Santo Tomàs prisoner-of-war camp in Manila or of Japanese executions of American pilots or that captured marines were tortured to death.

In an issue in 1944, we learned that in France, three of the world's greatest art treasures were hidden before the Nazis entered Paris: the *Mona Lisa*, the *Winged Victory*, and the *Venus de Milo*, and only twenty men knew the hiding place. We were simple children then—the kids on the block—and would hardly know of these art treasures.

News and images from the war front also affected fashion. Following the bombing of Pearl Harbor, Hawaii attained great importance as a military outpost for the United States, and newspapers, radio newscasts, and movie newsreels exploded with news about Hawaii. Newspaper featured black and white photos of the Hawaiian people, particularly women in hula skirts and leis, and suddenly, even we, the children on the block, were talking about Hawaii. In late summer, 1942, Helina and I decided to make hula skirts; we called them hula hula skirts. We scouted through the woods interspersed between the houses on our block and came across what might have been a mimosa tree, which bore straw colored seed pods, about six inches long, each pod containing several bean-like seeds. Sitting on Helina's stoop, with needle and thread, we sewed the long pods around a cord of some sort and made our hula hula skirts.

Despite being children, radio, newspapers, and the movies inevitably kept the somber mood of the war in us, clouding our childhood days. I felt like pushing the presence of war away, as if it were smoke, but war just imperiously superimposed itself everywhere on the atmosphere about me, whether I was on the sidewalk, in the woods, or at home.

Two specific wartime images left me with disturbing impressions. On one of our Saturday movie days, in a newsreel featuring the German army on parade, I saw the goose step for the first time and could not understand what seemed like an aberration of a regular marching step, something wrong with the leg from the knees down. Eventually, I learned that that manner of marching was called, "the goose step," and I identified it with Nazism and warfare brutality. I learned later that it had been in use much earlier in history, introduced by the Prussian army in the eighteenth century, devised for greater efficiency in training soldiers as well as virtuosic military display in formal military parades.

The other image haunting me I also saw in newsreels. I learned of the military decoration known as the Purple Heart, which the United States Armed Forces awarded to servicemen wounded in action. The newsreel would show the soldier with a missing limb or arm sitting in a wheelchair. As a young adolescent, seeing the limbless soldiers sitting in wheelchairs or struggling on crutches made me feel like shrinking away, and the evocation at night of their images frightened me.

As the war progressed, American society began to experience a somewhat chaotic shift in mood. Popular songs increasingly flooded the radio waves, and war-themed movies in a fever of creativity sought to boost America's morale. Frenzied social dances and live entertainment for the Armed Forces and their families provided in the different neighborhoods by the USO (United Service Organizations, chartered by the United States Congress) mingled strangely with the growing number of war fatalities, of awarded Purple Heart medals. The appearances of the Western Union messengers, whether on a bicycle or foot, with his fatal news to deliver seem to become more frequent, as did a gold star placed in a neighbor's house, indicating the death of a serviceman or perhaps, a service woman. Stranger still, a war-generated loosening of the moral structure of society began to take place, yes, a war-generated modified change of social conventions was stealthily overtaking American society.

The feel of the omnipresence of war on our lives was reinforced by the soldiers, sailors, and marines we encountered in our neighborhoods, likely on furlough. We saw the WACs (Women's Army Corps) and the WAVEs (Women Accepted for Volunteer Emergency Service, which was the women's branch of the United States Naval Reserve).

We were also aware of the USO, United Service Organization, established through President Roosevelt's order. The USO aimed to provide recreation to uniformed personnel and to boost morale. Aside from buildings assigned to hold USO activities, communities eager to hold their USO evenings, created clubs, held in adapted spaces as, in churches. We were too young to participate in the USO or make note of where in our community a USO evening might be held.

We saw older teen-age girls who appeared quite bold or more daring, dressing in a flashier style and becoming flirtatious when they encountered a serviceman. Perhaps they gained entrance to a USO hall and got as close to a serviceman as they could in dancing the fox trot. We were not aware that they were referred to as the "khaki-whacky *V* girls"– the soldier crazy victory girls.

The war boosted the economy, as wars tend to do, resulting in Americans having more cash in hand than they ever had before, if less items to purchase with it. Also, as wars tend to do, the war introduced a smack of hedonism, a "Gather-ye-roses-while-ye may" morality. One of the most dreaded words of the war, as even we children were aware of, was "overseas," or, "abroad," for, of course, the war front was there.

A soldier destined to be shipped overseas did not know if he would be blown to smithereens tomorrow; neither did his girlfriend or wife know. The prospect of death or being maimed or taken prisoner placed great emphasis on today, for who knew about tomorrow? Once overseas, a good number of men sought to avoid battle. Some broke down; some sought honorable discharges. The WACs and the WAVEs were also deployed overseas. Although they usually performed their duties far behind the front lines, a good number of women serving in the armed forces were killed in war-related accidents.

The temper of daily life rode higher. Hasty marriages took place, some shortly after ending in divorce. In some cases, frenzied dances and the romantically close dancing of the fox trot during the USO evenings, honoring and cheering the serviceman onward, became quite intimate, and along with war brides were the war betrayals.

Perhaps the best insight into the feel of the time could be gleaned from some of the wartime popular songs, revealing an awareness of the war's effect on morality and a shrewd Yankee humor obliquely admonishing the transgressor: "Johnny Doughboy Found a Rose in Ireland"; "Somebody Else Is Taking My Place"; "You Can't Say No to a Soldier"; "I'm Doin' It for Defense." The fidelity of the "Three Little Sisters," who respectively love a soldier, a sailor, and a marine and promise to stay home and read magazines, is questioned: "You can tell it to the soldier, tell it to the sailor and tell it to the Marines." From that song, "Tell it to the Marines," became a current catch phrase for bunk, which we too began to use. We heard the current popular songs with their underlying admonishments of a relaxing of conventions infusing America's war-gripped society but were too young to understand the frenzied war-goaded activities and the sexual innuendos of the very songs we sang.

For me, two songs epitomized the contrasting sentiments of the wartime era: one romantic and the other farcical. The romantic song, "Lili Marlene," struck both Axis and Allies soldiers with a wartime-ecstasy. The soldiers were mesmerized. They were filled with a yearning dream of love for a woman, Lili Marlene, who comes to a soldier standing beneath the lamppost by the barrack gate, waiting for her. (Translations of the original German into English vary. In the original German, Lili Marlene stands in front of the lamppost waiting for the soldier, who apparently addresses her from the abode of the dead.)

It is not hard to imagine soldiers, Axis or Allies, at the front, perhaps in a trench, perhaps on a desolate campsite, perhaps with wounded on a stretcher, awaiting medical help, all, feeling forlorn, disillusioned with war, nostalgic, thinking of home, wives, girlfriends. Then through the radio, they hear broadcast over the airways, from Radio Belgrade for the Axis soldiers, and from the Eighth Army, in North Africa, for the Allies, the sultry voice of a chanteuse singing "Lili Marlene." The mesmerizing voice sings in German to the Axis, and another mesmerizing voice sings to the Allies, in English translation. Not least contributing to the song's transfixing spell was the simple, haunting melody and catching chorus, with a dotted rhythm reverberating with folksong-like echoes from some Austrian village. And who were these spellbinding chanteuses? Lale Andersen, German chanson singer, and the incomparable, the ultimate in cosmopolitan sophistication, the legendary Marlene Dietrich, who sang "Lili Marlene" in German and, after her emigration to America, in English.

The song epitomizing the farcical vein was, "Don't sit under the apple tree with anyone else but me," particularly because of its image of an apple tree. What could be more American than an apple? Although written in wartime 1942, the colloquial feel of the song, the characteristic wry Yankee humor, and the fetching jaunty rhythm render it a classic in American popular songs.

At the time, the families on the block may not have been fully aware of the existence of concentration camps, at least not in our household. Italy and the plight of our relatives there were topics my sister Natalia and I occasionally overheard Mama and Papa discussing. Possibly, the German family who lived in the next house from us (between us was a good-sized woods) received a postcard or two from relatives in a Jewish ghetto, but the cards, like the letters that arrived at our house censored, revealed no crucial information. Another Jewish family of my acquaintance had received two postcards from relatives in a Jewish Ghetto in Poland, after which the relatives were never heard from again.

In April 1945, the United States Army entered Ohrdruf (a branch of Buchenwald), which became the first Nazi concentration camp liberated. The inhuman conditions at Ohrdruf exploded into publicity, drawing a visit from General Eisenhower, who cabled General George C. Marshall, Head of the Joint Chiefs of Staff, in Washington, describing the heinous conditions he had witnessed. He added that he made the visit deliberately to give "first-hand evidence . . . if ever, in the future, there develops a tendency to charge these allegations merely to 'propaganda.'"

Now, neighborhoods across the country learned of the atrocities, staring at black and white newspaper photos and possibly watching movie newsreels featuring prisoners who appeared like skeletal specters with haunting, hollow faces. During the war, while deeply affected emotionally by the mounting casualties of armed forces and civilians, we were made to understand that killing and maiming were the underpinnings of war. But that a systematic State-run—*State-run*—machine was created solely to kill human beings, by incinerating them, was unbelievable, a horror exacerbated by a scathing disgust upon learning the insidious, psychopathic ruse, as, for example, going on a vacation, to entice them to actually end up in a furnace! Despite vocabulary's extraordinary range of words and phrases to express human emotions and acts, here, vocabulary must reach an impasse, for recording such demonic events on histories' parchments would be so searing as to set them on fire.

As the war continued with its casualties, radio news broadcasts, and black-and-white movie newsreels, the children on the block, including myself, were reaching adolescence. The childhood tone was shifting from the Alice-in-Wonderland feel of the everyday and our faith in the little wonders each day would afford us. We felt a growing sense of a need for purpose, for a direction of energy toward more than play.

18

The Tragic Cost of Peace

By 1945, an increasing number of homes along the city blocks exhibited a gold star in front windows. More servicemen were coming home without a limb or an arm or two, and Johnny or Bobby could not come home because both arms and legs were amputated, leaving only a torso and sometimes part of a face. More servicemen who were afflicted with what we termed, *shell shock,* would never surmount the horror they witnessed, like one of our cousins, waking up screaming every night, plagued by horrific nightmares, and whose return to normal life was marred by irreparable mental damage.

Harrowing desperate acts haunt battlefields, as in the story of Gerald and Roy. Having fought on the Italian front, Gerald was one of those men waking up screaming. After a heavy bombing by the enemy, Gerald and his close army friend Roy were the only two men left on a battlefield strewn with dead bodies. Roy was on the ground, his entrails slipping out of his ripped open stomach. "Shoot me! Shoot me! Please, please! I'm finished. The pain is unbearable. Please! Please!" With trembling hands, Gerald fired the gun. Eventually, the war would be over, but every night, Gerald shoots his dear friend Roy and wakes up screaming.

In addition to the mental and physical injuries that accompanied soldiers upon their return home from the battlefield, there were other maladies with which they could be inflicted. Our cousin, Dominick, contracted malaria, presumably in the Pacific theater of war and was subject to relapses through the subsequent years.

Battles had followed one after another. In Italy, there were the battles of Salerno, Angio, and Montecassino, all part of the Italian campaign as the Allies moved north from Sicily. In France, the invasion of Normandy (D-Day) incurred a staggering number of Allied casualties and was paramount in changing the map of Europe from the insidious spread of Fascist-held territories to the heartening freedom of democracies.

Regrettably, that heartening freedom came at a tragic cost. Dresden, Germany, was pulverized by Allied bombings, resulting in the estimated deaths of twenty-five thousand people. In the Pacific theater of war, American forces—both the marines and the navy—did raise the American flag at Iwo Jima, but at the cost of a staggering number of casualties, with American casualties surpassing Japanese casualties. Also killed in the Pacific theater of war was the widely recognized journalist and war correspondent Ernie Pyle.

The Potsdam Declaration (issued on July 26, 1945) by the leaders of the United States, Great Britain, and China, calling for the unconditional surrender of Japan was rejected by the Japanese Supreme War Council (the Big Six). Yet within the Council, several members favored surrender, perhaps bearing in mind that five major cities, including Tokyo, had already been gutted by B-29s, and that there were a great number of deaths and wounded among the Japanese people.

In 1945, with the consent of the United Kingdom, the United

States dropped the first atomic bomb. After a seventy-five-hour interval (with the continuing demand for unconditional surrender), the United States dropped the second bomb, which had a greater power of destruction, causing physicists to grimly observe that the "improved" second bomb had already made the first one obsolete. We, the children, learned that the two bombs were called *atomic,* a nomenclature probably strikingly new to a good portion of the population. The dropping of the catastrophic bombs and the unspeakable devastation of two cities and annihilation of a tragic portion of the population overruled dissension within Japan's imperial government, prevailing upon it to surrender.

In "the first of the sort in Japanese History" (the *Daily News,* August 15, 1945), Emperor Hirohito delivered a radio broadcast to his people, at noon, on Wednesday, Tokyo time, Tuesday, New York time, appealing to them to submit to the surrender and ended his eloquently phrased appeal with, "Let the entire nation continue from generation to generation." He advised his people to, "Cultivate the ways of rectitude," to "Foster nobility of spirit . . . and keep pace with the progress of the world."

While people everywhere were initially thrilled by the prospect of peace, over time, for the full enormity of the two bombs' destruction, wrought by fission, was revealed progressively, they would very well be dismayed by the cost of that peace. Photos in newspapers and in *LIFE* magazine revealed the destroyed cities, clouds of smoke above and tracts of land laid waste. Even the pilots of the *Enola Gay* aircraft carrying the atomic bomb, exclaimed, "My God," when upon dropping it, they saw the giant deadly mushroom stem and a white billowy cloud leap on top of it to the height of twenty thousand feet, upon which the top of the cloud broke off and another cloud formed on the stem, all, carrying out the deadly chain reaction. Of Hiroshima, in one newspaper, the caption of a photo with two views was, "The City of the Dead."

On August 7, 1945, the day after the first bomb was dropped, the headline of *The Home News,* the daily paper covering the Bronx and Manhattan, read, "Great Atomic Devastation admitted by Japs; Tokyo terms bomb 'Destroyer of Mankind.'" In an article in the same edition, a reporter ponders if the "Atomic Age" will commence a "Golden Era or World's End."

Japan's formal unconditional surrender to the United States and its Allied powers took place aboard the battleship, *USS Missouri,* September 2, 1945. The war was over. We had entered the war in December 1941, and now, in August 1945, when Japan accepted full defeat, the war was over. The war was fought over the Atlantic, in air patrols and attacks to destroy the treacherous German U-boats. It was fought in North Africa: Ethiopia, Tunisia, Algeria. It was fought in Europe: Poland (by the Russians, referred to as the *Reds),* France, Britain, Italy, Germany. It was fought in Russia: Moscow, Stalingrad (by the Russians). It was fought in the Pacific (by the United States, which sought to avoid putting troops on Japan's shores, and briefly, by the Russians). It was a World War.

In times of peace and general goodwill, it is impossible to recreate the wartime state of mind of the populace, carrying on daily life with an underlying desperate wish for the war's ever-threatening, malefic presence to not be there, to evaporate, and to wake up tomorrow morning to the resumption of sweet normal life.

In times of peace and general goodwill, it is also impossible to recreate the wartime state of mind of the commanding ranks and the armed forces to accurately judge decisions made to conquer enemy forces under the pressing needs of the moment. They may well be thrust into a torturous unanswerable quandary about acts committed during the war. Were they justified? Were they wrong?

Many soldiers, years later, living in times of peace and goodwill, often find themselves revisiting and questioning decisions they made on the battlefield. My friend Jim, a soldier in World War II, on the Mediterranean Front, was one such soldier. His regiment had just fought a battle, and in the ensuing chaos, he and several other soldiers, stranded, hungry, dreadfully thirsty, unbathed for weeks, lice-ridden, feet blistered and muddied, boots worn, stumbled upon several German soldiers. They, too, were lost, and they raised their hands up in surrender. Like Jim and his fellow soldiers, they were young men, boys, with their whole lives ahead of them. Yet, Jim and his fellow soldiers were caught up in that moment of wartime desperation, in the perception of that anguishing moment in which war was life and death, and peace and everyday civilian life and decency no longer existed. In telling me the story years later, Jim hesitated, looked at me with eyes that once again saw that battlefield, and said, "We shot them."

In times of peace and within the world view of generations who did not live during that war, it is impossible to pronounce judgement on that regrettable action. In peacetime, even the American soldiers themselves, Jim and his fellow soldiers, now with families and nice homes, would probably not be able to face, with a clear conscience, that scene of gunshots and the young Germans soldiers falling to the ground.

Within a Fascist government, suspension of judgment might also be applied to the ordinary citizen, who, in the frenzy of war and caught up in zealous patriotism, betrays a neighbor, causing the neighbor's torture and death. After the war, in peacetime, the betrayer might not even comprehend his or her shameful betrayal. "How could I have!" The betrayer may very well live the rest of life with an anguishing sense of guilt never to be mediated by an answer to what is right or wrong in the abnormal state of war.

In war, there exists either victory or defeat, and immense suffering is shared on both sides. However, victory is often accompanied by celebration, despite the profound suffering on both sides. And so, at the end of World War II, in the eastern hemisphere, the two cities of Japan were aflame, burning with a cataclysmic fire and stricken with mounting fatalities. There, the populace was filled with mortal terror at the chains of fires, the ravaging of their neighborhoods, the mounting dead on the once peaceful streets. In the western hemisphere, ours, the populace rejoiced. They were deeply thankful for the end of devastating battles and of the countless soldiers who drowned or were slain on beachheads, in war-decimated cities, and in dense, dangerous jungle-like territories. Added to that were some four million civilian casualties, including the Holocaust victims. The populace, grateful for peace, though afflicted with a sad, undying remembrance of the fatalities and horrors of war inflicted on all people, however caught up in war denotations such as Allies or Axis, was moved to hold celebrations. On the New York City blocks, including ours, Eastville Avenue, neighbors held block parties, and hopped and twirled, Helina and I among them, to that jubilant thirties and forties dance music, jitterbug.

The war had concluded, and the twentieth century sped on into the twenty-first century, held fast by the brilliant hold of technology. The populace could now find some reassurance, supported by the prevalence of democracy on the European continent (no longer tread on by the goose step), secured from the travails of World War II. That heavy feeling of war pervading the city blocks, invading the minds of adults, and of us, somewhere in the peripheries of our mind, seemingly like a shroud, a veiled menacing thing no one could shoo away has dissipated, dissolved in the ever-passing motion of human time.

This generation, which had conquered Fascism in Europe, was designated The Greatest Generation. This generation, my generation, is vanishing, even as I am now, though not without lasting memories. I see the children on the block collecting newspapers for the war effort. I hear the siren and see streams of searchlights moving across the night skies. I see soldiers or a WAC or WAVE walking along our block, and in newsreels, soldiers with missing limbs or arms. I see my cousin, a lieutenant, ready to embark for the dreaded overseas, where the battles were taking place, as his wife weeps. I recall a composition we were assigned in fifth grade, entitled, "The Stormtroopers Are Coming." I see Mama laden with shopping bags and placing blue or red tokens or paper ration stamps on the counter, along with money. I hear the anthems of the armed forces—the Halls of Montezuma.

We, The Greatest Generation, now, a vanishing generation.

Part Five

Letters from Aunt Raffaella

19

Fate of Family in Italy

THE WAR also ended in Europe. The immigrant families on our block, including the Germans, Helina's Polish family, the Czechoslovakians (as the country was called then), and the Italian families now hoped to receive uncensored letters and learn of the plight of their relatives in Europe. Soon, we were buying onionskin airmail envelopes and letter paper. Called onionskin because of its resemblance to the very thin outer layers of an onion, the envelopes had short diagonal red and blue lines along the border, and the letter paper was thin, strong, and transparent.

After the war, our German Jewish neighbors received no communication from their relatives abroad. During the war, their relatives were told to pack in preparation for a trip. They packed casual clothes and a dressy outfit or two, including some jewelry, for a possible festive occasion, and they made sure to put their house key in a secure place in the suitcase for their return. As it happened, as much as these neighbors yearned to buy that airmail onionskin stationery to communicate once again with their beloved relatives, there was no need.

Uncensored letters now began to arrive at our house from Aunt Raffaella, Mama's sister, my godmother, whom I introduced earlier in these reminiscences. Unhappily, the very bright, and spirited adolescent, Raffaella, promising to develop into the handsome young women characteristic of her family lineage, was struck with a mysterious (at that time) disease, which stunted her growth and left her slightly humped. The cause had never been determined, though her sister Annina had attributed it to dampness––the stone houses, the cobblestone streets, the moist all-encompassing sirocco wind sweeping up from the Ionian Sea, plunging the entire city of Montevetuso into a ghostly hallucination, its macabre whirling mists enveloping the cathedral's campanile, the clock tower, anybody caught in its sweeping embrace.

When she was young, she expected to grow into the lovely line of women her family was known for, like her two sisters. In that period of changing girlish form, how naïve she was, expecting dainty breasts filling lace-trimmed dresses and blouses, a slenderizing waistline curving gracefully into hips, shapely legs like Annina's. Instead, her stricken body had come forth with breasts not knowing where to go in the shortened stature but right down to the waist, hips that did not have room enough to curve gently, legs, shortened with barely room for the suggestion of an ankle.

Who can fathom the torment that Raffaella endured as she grew and became aware of her abnormally developing body? Nevertheless, a malevolent disease could not subdue the fiery will beneath whatever form her body took. Raffaella was not going to be gripped by some fatal nemesis. With towering willpower—perhaps the power of rage—she became a brilliant schoolteacher. Perhaps on that first day of teaching in the elementary school, seeing this not quite normal stature of a teacher, the children gawked or tittered, but she had to simply speak in her impeccable Italian, and she was in command. Eventually, she gained renown in the city and became known to all as *La Signorina*. Parents hoped that their child would be placed in her class, because a teacher carried the same class all through the elementary school years.

Aunt Raffaella had notified Papa and Mama of their mothers' death during the long war. Black-bordered envelopes arrived on Eastville Avenue, each with its announcement of a death in the family, and for each, Papa and Mama, the death of a mother, drawing from them an anguishing pain, all the more because they were three thousand miles away and could not be at the bedside of their dying mother. They were well aware of the customs in Italy: the family would paste black-bordered paper announcements on walls in the city; the church would toll its number of bells for the death of a woman—four slowly repeated tolls followed by two closing gongs (five tolls for the death of a man); and, if it were summer, the family would close the French doors giving onto a front balcony, indicating that there was a death in the family.

With the war now behind them, one of the first crucial pieces of news that Aunt Raffaella informed Mama of was that their two brothers—my uncles—were home, safe and sound. In the war, one brother was stationed in the South, the other in the North, under the *nazifascista* controlled part of Italy, from Rome upward. When the South surrendered and joined the Allies, theoretically, the brothers became enemies of each other. During the war, the brother in the South would not point his gun at a single soldier in the North, lest he shot his own brother (as he revealed after the war).

Raffaella added that Papa's family members who lived in Genoa also emerged unscathed. As Italy's largest port city, Genoa had been heavily bombed by the Allies.

Continuing her narrative regarding the fate of our relatives, Raffaella wrote of what happened to our cousin Lucia. The sad event took place in 1943, during the war. Lucia and her family lived in Rome, not far from Vatican City, in a handsome house with an elaborate iron-wrought balcony in front and a small iron-wrought balcony on the side, off Lucia's bedroom. At that time, Lucia was an attractive modest girl of about sixteen years old. Looking out her side balcony, Lucia would see the convent next door, which housed the order of discalced Carmelite nuns, who wore white habits. The convent had an open colonnaded cloister where the nuns could be glimpsed as they strolled in it, praying, and she would gaze at the sisters longingly, yearning to join them.

When Lucia turned seventeen years old, she begged her parents to permit her to join the Carmelite nuns next door, but her parents refused, unwilling to have their daughter pursue a cloistered religious life. Desperate, more than once, Lucia stole away from home, knocked at the great paneled double front doors of the convent, and begged the nuns to take her in. Eager to give her refuge for the moment, the nuns welcomed her, but Lucia's mother, who knew where her daughter had gone, would not hear of Lucia entering the Order and each time, fetched her and conducted the weeping daughter home.

On one sultry summer night, with a gentle breeze caressing the air, wearing a white flared chiffon peignoir over her loose white cotton crepe nightgown, Lucia stole away again to the convent, and avoiding the great paneled double front doors, made her way through the open cloister, unlatched a gate, and rushed into the convent. Her peignoir, with its loose, flared sleeves, billowed behind her, and her hair flowed freely, all carried by the soft breeze. One of the nuns, happening to be within the confines, perhaps to close the door to the cloister for the night, in a sudden transported moment of religious ecstasy, thought she saw a dove, with stunning outstretched wings flying into the convent from the cloister and called out, *"un colombo!"* (a dove—easily called to mind because a white dove is a symbol of the Holy Spirit). Hearing the call, all the nuns rushed to the cloister entrance and gazed in astonishment at Lucia, she herself remaining fixed, her arms still open, as in a passing shock at her escapade. Early the next morning, discovering Lucia's disappearance and knowing that she had once again stolen to the convent, Lucia's mother finally conceded to her daughter's request to join the Order.

Upon becoming nuns, women took new names, saint names, to symbolize the holy life to which they were now dedicated. The Carmelite Order decided that Lucia keep her Baptismal name, Lucia. Santa Lucia is sometimes represented holding her eyes on a tray, either gouged out by a persecutor or by her, she herself, to discourage a suitor who admired them. When she was prepared for burial, apparently, her eyes had been miraculously restored. Saint Lucia is also associated with light: the root *luc, lux,* in Latin, and is the patron saint of the blind.

Lucia would now be called Suora (Sister) Lucia. As much as the Carmelites venerated Santa Lucia, they always referred to Sister Lucia as *la Suora Columbina,* the Sister Little Dove—the diminutive, *Columbina,* indicating endearment. Once entering the convent, Sister Little Dove never emerged from the convent and was not henceforth glimpsed in the cloister, but that was not for religious reasons.

On August 14, 1943, Rome was declared an "Open City," but prior to that date and after, the Allies heavily bombed parts of Rome, and a thousand or so Italian civilians were killed. One day, an Allied bomb hit the convent, demolishing the building, and killing all the Carmelites, including the Little Dove Nun.

20

Fascist Youth

RAFFAELLA'S LETTERS also informed Mama of the changing political conditions in Italy after the war ended. She wrote about the fate of the King of Italy, Victor Emmanuel III, and the drastic changes in Italy's form of government. Having lived in Italy for a good part of their lives, Papa and Mama were already familiar with some of the content of Aunt Raffaella's letters, but background is needed in my narrative of events.

Victor Emmanuel had initially been well-liked by his people. He was affectionately referred to as both the "little saber," since he was only five feet tall, and as "the Soldier King" for sustaining kingship through both world wars. He held Italy's throne from 1900 to 1946, when he abdicated in favor of his son Umberto, who reigned for only one month because in 1946, in a public referendum, Italy voted to become a republic. The people eventually turned against Victor Emmanuel for his weakness in controlling the dictatorial designs of the now hated Mussolini. Among the reasons why the king persisted in supporting Mussolini was that Mussolini's command was a stronghold, substantiated by his special armed squads, the feared Blackshirts (the *Camicie nere)*, against the Communists, whom the king looked upon as his enemy.

In one of her letters, reflecting on the effect of the harsh regime of Mussolini on the lives of children, Aunt Raffaella conceded that as much as she wanted her sister Annina and godchild Annalisa and her new, unknown niece Natalia, close to her, she was grateful we were in America, out of the cruel grip of fascism. She wrote of the rigorous disciplinary rules controlling the lives of children. Children, from eight to fourteen years old, were obliged to enroll in the *Opera Nazionale Balilla*, the youth wing of the National Fascist Party. Girls wore the regulated white blouse and black skirt (as Mama did), and the older girls also wore a black tie. Boys wore the regulated fascist gray green pants and black shirts. The children learned the fascist raised arm salute, supposedly modeled on the Roman salute of antiquity, and later adopted by the Nazis. (Hitler took good notice of Mussolini's techniques and utilized them for his own purposes). The children learned slogans adulating Il Duce (Mussolini) and sang "Giovanezza," the fascist official hymn, on every public occasion. In post-World War II, "Giovanezza" was banned.

During school recess, among other paramilitary types of activities, boys were taught to march while holding muskets. If parents protested having a son enrolled in the *balilla,* the teacher would inform them that their son could not attend school. The *balilla* also prescribed exercises for girls to develop their physical agility, while the exercises for boys were geared towards training them to be soldiers. The *balilla* preceded the Nazi Youth of Germany and perhaps served as a model.

Far indeed was this vise-like grip of Fascism on Italy from the life of Annalisa, Natalia, and Helina playing their sidewalk games on Eastville Avenue. They were in sweet innocence of the menacing presence of Mussolini's violent Squadristi patrolling the streets to root out townspeople suspected of having Socialist or Communist persuasions. The Squadristi, also known as the Blackshirts, was a voluntary militia of the Italian Fascist Party (perhaps a forerunner of the later German Stormtroopers), given to uncontrolled violence, attacking even trade unions, Catholics, and people adhering together in cooperatives.

On the cobblestone streets of Montevetuso, if a child saw a Blackshirt on his patrolling walk, the child would have been instructed by his parents that if he were greeted, he should smile and answer politely, with, "Buon giorno." Clearly, if a child showed any form of animosity, the child's family would be suspected of dissension.

Under these macabre circumstances, there would hover in the air a continual sense of menace, which children (as Raffella, a schoolteacher, knew), would astutely discern, for they have an instinctive awareness of what could be dangerous. They would be aware of parents and relatives conversing in whispers and know that they were discussing alarming local incidents. They would probably also intuit the underlying fear and panic in their parents' expressions and behavior, such as hiding behind curtains and gazing frequently outside the windows of the rooms.

Children would later learn about appalling incidents, about the deadly arrest of neighbors, often at midnight (of course). Typically, the house would be invaded by the *fascisti*, knocking or breaking down the door, roughly grabbing a terrified man, witnessed by his terrified family members, and dragging him out into the big black car. He would never be heard from again.

It was said that if one were brought before the Fascist authorities, it would be better to claim that you were Jewish. This would lead to confinement in an Italian concentration camp, which was more humane than camps in Germany and Poland, until Hitler took over Central and Northern Italy. Then the Germans, with the collaboration of Italian police and Fascists (whether in the line of duty of not), sent substantial numbers of Italian Jews to Auschwitz. (Mussolini was anticlerical, and one of his mistresses, Ines Sarffati was Jewish. Under the yoke of Hitler, he changed policies.) The Fascist authorities were excessively brutal in their treatment of antifascists and particularly the hated Communists, who were a major force in the Italian Resistance.

In 1943, Southern Italy surrendered to the Allies and became part of Allied forces. Consequently, in Southern Italy and Montevetuso, Fascism was overthrown and could now be openly despised and cursed. The Blackshirts of Montevetuso could not rid themselves fast enough of the now treacherous uniforms. Burn them! Shred them! Bury them! Literally overnight, a citizen in a black shirt would emerge in civilian clothes and take every opportunity to express approbation of the new regime, of being united in the war effort with *gli americani.*

Many Blackshirts were town residents, some even neighbors of Aunt Raffaella. In Montevetuso, a relatively small walled hill city, the populace knew all particulars relating to the townspeople, if not as neighbors, through gossip or rumors. They knew that some among the Blackshirts loathed Fascism but had to become a Fascist to obtain a job or keep one or not to have their children taunted by children of Blackshirts or perhaps refused entrance to the elementary school. These neighbors were readily reintegrated back into society, a society that could scarcely believe in its new freedom, which was like a dream they feared they would awaken from.

In every culture, there exists individuals of questionable reputation, disgruntled men estranged from society. At that time, some disgruntled soldiers and idle, troublesome youth who saw in the *camicie nere,* an opportunity to reinvest themselves in some role in society. Oh, to don a uniform, which imbued them with a sense of power, to strut along the cobblestone streets and strike fear into the people! Now, let the people dare defy them, in their black uniform!! Naturally, the Fascist paramilitary force heartily welcomed them knowing they would be staunchly loyal to Il Duce and his Fascist empire. Of the number of Fascists in Montevetuso, one, in particular, arrogant and always threatening, was loathed by the townspeople. They referred to him as *la bestia*.

Upon the downfall of Fascism in Southern Italy, *la bestia*, knew he had to flee Montevetuso but had no time to devise a plan. A small band of men, some, family men, good citizens, had already started the pursuit. As Aunt Raffaella wrote "He ran over the roofs of houses, down alleys, into the labyrinth, and finally, desperately, he climbed up onto the city wall to jump. But the pursuing men caught him, and with their bare hands and some tools—*l'hanno ammazzato! ammazzato! ammazzato!*"

The harshness of the *mm* and *zz* of that onomatopoeic word, *ammazzato,* to kill violently, to beat to death, brought to Mama and Papa reading the letter a shuddering vision of that gory scene. Had I, by then a young teenager, lived on in Italy, I, of course, would not see that bludgeoned body but would bear the memory of that violent occurrence and the knowledge of the possible brutality of a wrathful citizenry as well as of a brutal enemy. How unlikely in my childhood days in the Bronx was the possibility of such an image being stored within the inner reaches of my memory.

21

White Widows

IN ONE OF her letters to Mama, Aunt Raffaella mentioned the deaths of Francesca and Angela, whom Mama knew in her childhood. Mama referred to them as "white widows," *le vedove bianche*. What was a white widow, I asked, and learned about a striking phase in the history of Southern Italy.

The term, *white widow,* was specific to Southern Italy, particularly during the mass migrations of Southern Italians to America from the 1890s through the 1920s.

The white widows did not wear black because their husbands were not deceased. They were in the Americas or Switzerland or Germany or Northern Italy to find employment and send money home to their families in the perennially poor Southern Italian cities, like Montevetuso. The marriage of some white widows was adversely affected by their husbands' migration, causing them to look upon North America, as *la mala femmina,* a bad woman luring men away from their families, a femme fatale. *L'America* was a *terra maledetta,* a cursed land, whose infected air made men forget their past life in Italy and their homes. Crossing the Atlantic, they might as well have crossed Lethe, the river of forgetfulness.

Perhaps America was truly a femme fatale. Perhaps the men, including my maternal grandfather (a fine carpenter who did have employment in Montevetuso), emigrating to America ostensibly for better employment opportunities, felt within themselves a tingling excitement about setting forth onto the great Atlantic and meeting the challenges of the New World. Perhaps even my grandmother, who refused to emigrate, thought of America as a *mala femmina,* for America had lured her daughter Annina away, with her newborn baby Annalisa, whom she held in her arms a mere six months. America had lured her husband away twice, each time for a good number of years, as he found employment in a piano factory. (She bore her fifth and final child twenty-five years after her firstborn, Raffaella, ten years older than her sister Annina). When my grandfather finally returned to resume his life in Montevetuso, it's possible that the femme fatale did continue to haunt him. From time to time, he may have been overwhelmed by strong yearnings to set forth once more across the great ocean, on to America.

Like my grandmother, Francesca refused to emigrate to America with her husband Stefano, but he decided that he would fulfill his dreams anyway. Stefano was a skilled shoemaker, but in Montevetuso, where much of the population was poor (clergy, teachers, and sparse nobility being the exception), he could not practice his art of making fine shoes. Ordinarily, he simply mended shoes, which rendered him little beyond mere sustenance.

In America, specifically New York City, Stefano became prosperous. He sent a generous stipend to his wife Francesca regularly, and a pair of elegant high-laced white leather shoes, which made a sensation in Montevetuso, as did the gramophone he sent, which astounded and delighted Francesca's family and friends. Although waves of nostalgia for his beloved natal city overwhelmed him at times, Stefano made no immediate preparations to return to Italy. He was thriving in New York City and knew that however much he wanted to be reunited with his good wife Francesca and his dear little son Domenico, who had been but one-year-old when he left for America, in Montevetuso, he would revert mostly to mending shoes with pittance for wages. In New York City, he was a craftsman and well paid. Besides, Stefano loved the excitement of being in a foreign land, among foreign peoples, and always in wonder at foreign customs. It would be hard to say whether the good money or excitement of a foreign port of call prolonged the moment of return to Italy.

Stefano remained in New York City for twenty years.

When Stefano finally returned to Montevetuso and stepped on his threshold, the woman he saw was not the young wife he remembered. Similarly, Francesca did not see the young dashing man she remembered. Francesca, whose hair was flecked with gray and showed fine lines at the corner of her eyes, looked attractive in her simple blue dress with a white lace collar and lace trim on the long sleeves, but with her waistline thickened and merging into hips, she had lost her once shapely figure. Yet, Francesca's altered appearance was not as drastic as that of Stefano, who lost most of his hair. Francesca also noted that he had put on considerable weight and surmised that foods were plentiful in America and easily available.

In Italy, Stefano's diet consisted of pasta, vegetable, varieties of beans, often, lentils, and fruit. Meat was expensive and used sparingly, mostly at festival times, and a small portion of pastry cost more than a loaf of bread. In America, his diet included butter as well as olive oil, meat almost daily, at times, a pastry, and American ice cream, which is richer than gelato.

In any case, after a migration that practically amounted to emigration, here was her husband, standing diffidently on the threshold, uncertain of his welcome. Ushering Stefano into his own house, Francesca treated him like a guest, though soon enough the awareness grew upon her that he was here to stay. They were husband and wife. Husband and wife? She had become accustomed to life without him. She had become an independent woman, managing all the household needs and repairs, a proper upbringing of Domenico, and worked on a small piece of land she and Stefano owned outside the city walls. Resourcefully, she had budgeted Stefano's generous stipend, separating sums for expenditures on necessities and comforts and putting sums of money aside as savings. She felt that, subsequently, she could adequately carry on without his stipend. If she lived in the twenty-first century, she might have designated herself as a single parent. However, Francesca simply looked upon the circumstances that thrust her into the situation of a long-absent husband and of greatly increased responsibilities as the course of destiny.

After several perplexing days, as both floundered to restyle their lives as husband and wife, Francesca, who now resented not the twenty-year absence but the disruption of Stefano's return, faced him squarely and asked the question her resentment could not repress.

"Why did you return at all?"

"This is my country. I did not want to die in a foreign country." Stefano paused; perhaps he himself was wondering where twenty years had fled. "I wanted to return to my family."

There was someone in the household who wouldn't have felt too much regret if Stefano had died in a foreign country. Stefano's son Domenico, no longer a one-year-old coddling baby but a young man with opinions of his own, greeted his father respectfully but with little warmth. Domenico resented Stefano. He perceived him as an intruder into his mother's warm, secure household, enlivened with the constant visiting of relatives and friends.

In time, Domenico came to accept his father. Stefano had traveled to America, which would impress any son, and he could relate personal experiences in that country that tantalized the imagination of all the young men of Montevetuso.

With time, Stefano also settled into his marriage. Likewise, Francesca resumed what was then called her "marital duties," if moderated by aging and a strong sense of independence, so that the word, *duty*, attained greater relevance to the activity than in the first romantic glows of marriage.

Despite any estrangement Francesca might have felt from her husband, their marriage remained ostensibly intact. This was partly due to the larger communal roles of married men and women in the gregarious society of Montevetuso. Women socialized with women, as they filled their amphoras with water at the various water fountains, which was a type of café for women, a good place to socialize and exchange news and gossip, then walking home together, usually leaning their amporas against one hip or carrying them supported on their head. As with the ancient Greeks, amphoras were also receptacles for olive oil and wine.

Men would drop by a bar (café) for an espresso to socialize, and there was always the men's club for playing cards or engaging in other activities. During the passeggiata hour, men promenaded with men, some arm in arm, expressing male friendship, in accordance with the current concept of propriety. Women socialized together on balconies watching those below or would promenade supportively with an elderly relative, relieving the relative's reclusive days. Mothers might promenade with marriageable daughters, with the implicit intention of eyeing a possible suitor, also engaging in the passeggiata.

In time, as Aunt Raffaella informed Mama, Francesca died,

though she had been preceded by Stefano, and became a widow again, but not a *white widow*.

Angela, the other white widow Raffaella mentioned, was awaiting her betrothed Alfredo, a mason who had been working in New York City for two years and expected to return soon and marry her. True to his word, Alfredo returned and proposed marriage. The day of the wedding was the happiest day in Angela's life.

"She wore a beautiful silk white gown with a long train," recalled Cristina, a stocky woman who always wore a black dress, who had twenty-five of Arguses' one hundred eyes, who knew everything that happened in Montevetuso, and who was facetiously called the mayor of Montevetuso.

"She made the dress herself," continued Cristina. "All of us on via S. Rocco watched her as she walked slowly from her house to Saint Rocco's church, next door. She looked like a *principessa*."

Several months after their marriage, however, Alfredo informed his happy bride that he decided to return to New York City, where construction was booming, and he could make good money. "Who is building houses or schools or *grattacieli* in Montevetuso?" he reasoned with Angela, impressing her with his urgent work in the dynamic New World. He did not ask Angela to join him, but, as Angela knew, many husbands emigrated first and in time, summoned their wives. In any case, Angela resigned herself to becoming one of the white widows of Montevetuso.

Although America was more than three thousand miles away, men voyaging there, meeting one another in Lower Manhattan, and then returning, plus letters sailing across the Atlantic to Montevetuso, constituted an amazingly efficient source of information. Cristina first heard the news and rushed to see Angela.

"Did you know, Angela," Cristina exclaimed, "Alfredo has another wife in America!"

Angela stared unbelievingly at Cristina. Then she burst into tears; "How could he—!" And she began to sob. "Ruined, everything is ruined!"

If the ubiquity of relatives and friends in Montevetuso occasionally got on one's nerves, in times of misfortune, they made up a helpful support system. They rallied around the inconsolable Angela.

"You should be glad," they assured her. "Not to be the real wife of such a deceitful man, is the better condition to be in," though no one could figure out who, between the two, was the real wife.

Not long after the shocking revelation, Angela was just leaving her house when there before her stood Alfredo!

"You! You—!" Overcome by rage, anguish, for she still felt strongly for Alfredo, and a quivering sense of helplessness, she pulled off the wedding ring she still wore, flung it at him, stormed back into the house, and slammed the door.

Half of Montevetuso heard of this fiery episode, but being pragmatic and always contending with Southern Italy's *miseria*, they shook their heads disapprovingly. They had more practical solutions.

"She should have kept the ring, had it set with a jewel, and worn it," remarked many young women. Being indigent or hoping for suitors, who instead were emigrating to *l'America*, they wondered if they would ever wear a ring of any sort. Cristina bluntly remarked, "She should have sold the ring and kept the money."

At the men's club, the incident took on a different tone. Toni, voicing the consensus, said, "If Angela had a brother, he would fix that Don Giovanni up so that no woman would ever look at him again.

Angela remained in the peculiar state of being married and unmarried. She had no need to consider reverting to her maiden name, since upon marriage, Italian women do not take their husband's surname. She never sought another husband but lived quietly with her unmarried sister on via S. Rocco, making her living as a dressmaker. As Aunt Raffaella had informed Mama, Angela died. Alfredo was never heard of again, lost in the skyscraper world of New York City.

22

Aunt Raffaella's Death

In 1992, Aunt Raffella died at the age of ninety-two. Perhaps as she drifted away, she thought back to memorable and happy moments in her difficult life. She didn't want to dwell on her tormented adolescence and her body's alarmingly unnatural growth. Now at the end of life, perhaps she thought of her beloved father—my grandfather. She would have smiled, recalling how he reverently constructed two stools for her to stand on to reach a higher shelf in a kitchen cabinet or in the wardrobe in the bedroom. The purpose of the stool, however, that rendered her most grateful to her father, was to place the stool under the high kitchen window, to look at familiar sites of her beloved birth city and straining over the wide windowsill, to watch the activities of the people below as they carried out their busy lives.

Continuing to reminisce, Raffaella perhaps recalled the canary her father gave her. Oh! Even now, she hears the sweet trilling song of that fabled canary.

My grandfather bred song canaries, and through the rooms of my family house, could always be heard the sweet golden trills and silvery twittering of canaries. Years ago, awaiting a teaching position, Raffaella worked in the post office, which in those days, was located right across from her house, on Piazza Roma. One day, she had a novel idea.

"Papà," she said, "may I have a canary to bring to the post office? It will sing for us while we work."

Like Hans Christian Anderson's fabled nightingale, the canary my grandfather chose enchanted everyone who heard it. When its golden song filled the post office, employees selling stamps smiled and felt transported to tropical gardens, the handyman sweeping the floor leaned on his broom and listened, and the delivery man stopped still, forgetting to unload his package. Listening to the canary's cascades, the townspeople did not mind standing in line before the counter to send their letters and packages, some going to Switzerland or Germany where families emigrated to find employment. Others listened as they picked up packages from relatives in America, for it was common that those who emigrated to America sent packages to their much poorer relatives in Montevetuso. Townspeople, who had no reason for going to the post office, stopped by throughout the day to catch its song.

Raffaella faithfully fed the canary, and since she herself could not resist sugar in any form, even out of the sugar bowl, gave it pinches of sugar, which it happily pecked away, and as she felt sweetened its song. After her father died, Raffaella always kept a canary in her household and would feed her canary sugar. Unhappily, in the post office, the canary's gold spell turned malevolently against itself. Raffaella was so enchanted by its song, especially through the cold days of winter when its tropical trills evoked the campagna with fruit trees all in bloom, that she forgot to give it water for several days.

To her father's outrage and sorrow, and her own deep remorse, the fabled canary died. Yet, Listen! Like the phoenix, the canary has spread its wings anew and flown from the now long-gone post office a few feet across the piazza, back to my grandfather's canary room, and its lilting song is among the sounds trilling into eternity.

As she listens to the canary's song, she feels a deep peaceful sleep descending upon her. But no! Every year, Raffaella's sister Annina would visit her and spend the summer with her before returning to America. With her quasi-supernatural perseverance, Rafaella was determined not to die until Annina, due at any moment, arrived. Before long, Annina was there at her bedside, holding her hand. "Annina," Rafaella whispered, "Annina," and she smiled and closed her eyes.

Two sisters, two heroic women, two continents. Mama, braving departure from her beloved family to sail to a land, the New World, she knew nothing about, and to live with a husband she barely knew except for a few months of courtship. Yet, enterprising, unresistingly adapting to changes in customs, she made the most of a long life, despite never having a chance in that New World to rise to the level of the cultured woman she was in Italy. She remained that foreign woman with an Italian accent. Very well! Nothing would daunt her bright spirit, open to all that life would offer her, in the Old World or the New World.

Raffaella tenaciously drove her thwarted life ahead. She was the first inhabitant of Montevetuso to buy a television and welcome neighbors to wondrously view this mysterious machine in which people talked and moved, miraculously, set right there in *La Signorina's* parlor. Having adopted one of her nieces, Raffaella bought her an automobile and arranged for driving lessons. Her niece became the first woman driver in Montevetuso. She commissioned a painting to hang on the walls of Montevetuso's cathedral. *La Signorina* became the queen of Montevetuso. Yet, I recollect a moment when Mama, I, and Raffaella, sat at a table eating the midday dinner, engaging in some reminiscing conversation. Suddenly, Raffaella said, "When I was a young girl

—" and then she stopped, and tears came into her eyes. My aunt, Raffaella, an inspiring figure, for me, for all. No, no harsh fate would hold that indomitable will within its fatal grip, despite that telltale tear at our dinner. She was queen of Montevetuso. She was queen of life itself.

Raffaella was gathered up in Montevetuso's cemetery and buried in a private stone chapel with a cornice, a scrolled pediment, and a marble column on either side. On the cornice are inscribed the words she or her mournful siblings put together:

Memorie e lacrime,
Preghiere e speranze.

Part Six

The Vanishing Generation

23

Perspectives on a Mountaintop City

HAD I not emigrated but continued to live in a small, isolated ancient city on a mountaintop, I would have grown up within a milieu incorporating me with different perspectives of space and time.

My conception of distances, traversed by walking or by horse and carriage, would have been substantially different from that of living in the Bronx, where we took a long walk to school, to and from, four times a day, and, on occasion, rode in trolley cars, buses, or trains. Reminiscing about her life in Montevetuso, Mama would recall her family's picnics on a parcel of land they owned, far-off, in the "country." "As we sat and ate our picnic," she reminisced, "we would hear the *lucertole* [lizards] rustling in the grasses around us." That far-off land in the country was simply a good walk of fifteen minutes or so from the family's house on Piazza Roma, down the mountainside, at that time, a grassy plain running toward the base of the mountain. Even up to the twentieth century, some of the older townswomen in Montevetuso would say to me, "Have you seen our city walls far off?" That distance was a mere fifteen-minute walk or so from Piazza Roma to the encircling wall on top of the mountain.

Later in the twentieth century, Mama's country site was developed into the "new town," characteristic today of some hill towns in Italy, with the "old town" higher up the mountain and the modern "new town" below. Some families kept their ancient houses in the labyrinth but moved into the new town, installed with modern equipment.

One dimension a childhood in Montevetuso would have given me, which would hardly be conceivable on Eastville Avenue, is a sense of antiquity, of history, not in schoolbooks but there, in front of my eyes. Along Corso della Repubblica, I would have come upon the pre-eleventh-century Benedictine Abbey with its (legendary) three hundred and sixty-five rooms, some underground, one for each day of the year. On other walks, I would have passed such churches as the fifteenth-century Santa Lucia and Santa Stefano. Closer to my house, I would have walked past the Norman constructed palazzo with a battlement, on top of which is a parapet and crenels, giving the building a laced look.

In school (at that time, held in the ancient abbey), I would have learned about the location of the ancient city gates. The entrance gate to the city no longer existed, but part of the second gate at the top of the mountain remained intact, a great arched opening in the walls, flanked by columns. In ancient times, at the strike of a gong signaling two hours of night, the gates were closed against marauders. Standing at the opening of the second gate, one beheld far, far vistas of rolling land, its very silence summoning up tomes of ancient history, of the Odyssey, the Trojan War, of Aeneas and the founding of Rome. The only gate I would see in my purview of the Bronx was the gate on the school chain-link fence, and perhaps the only vestiges I would see of the far past might be the long-living trees in our woods—the maples, oaks, aspens, ashes, and horse chestnuts.

My daily scenes in Montevetuso would have differed widely from those on Eastville Avenue. I would have seen peasant women, always dressed in all black (except for that flashing gold earring), carrying out their chores. These women were well-versed in folklore as old as the fields they worked under Southern Italy's blazing sun in the feudalistic system still prevailing at that time. They held their own school, passing folk wisdom orally from generation to generation.

Despite the harsh period of fascism, there would have been happy times for a child growing up in Montevetuso. No, there would have been no Saturday movies or weekly radio programs, which constituted some of the activities of my life on Eastville Avenue, but Montevetuso had its own delights for children, such as the festivals celebrating the Madonna or saints. Two such events, the festival of the patron saint, Saint Rocco, in mid-August, and the feast of Epiphany, on 6 January are historically amongst the most celebrated and anticipated.

On the eve of Epiphany, the good witch, la Befana, rides through the sky on her broom, descends into houses, via the chimney, and leaves gifts for the children. These might typically be sweetmeats but a lump of coal or garlic if a child were bad. Versions of the Befana folklore differ, according to regions in Italy. La Befana may put the gifts in stockings hung on a mantelpiece or a big sock placed near a window or in shoes as well as stockings.

What I might have received in the 1930s, along with my young friends, could very well have been some fig dolls—dried figs, perhaps roasted, and stuffed with an almond, strung on cane in the shape of a doll or of a conifer tree. Perhaps my sock or stocking would include small egg-shaped honey drops, similar to ones Mama made Natalia and me when we had colds; a lost recipe involving honey and perhaps sugar, stirred continuously in a frying pan. Perhaps La Befana would also include a new graph paper notebook, which children used to keep their letters and numbers straight, in accordance with the historic script typical of Italian handwriting.

On Eastville Avenue, in bountiful America, at Christmas, slippers, pajamas, wool mittens, or perhaps a coveted Waterman fountain pen would sit in boxes under the Christmas tree. One year, Natalia and I received a small red phonograph with diminutive records playing light, well-known classical songs, such as Mendelssohn's "On Wings of Song," and "Sweet and Low," a musical setting of a poem by Lord Alfred Tennyson. Yet, it was not the elaborateness of the gifts or the quantity but the quality of the feeling of joy that made up the festivity and was the essence of Christmas, and in Italy, the feast of the Epiphany. Annalisa, in Montevetuso, would have been just as happy with her fig doll or a new home-knit pair of stockings as both Natalia and I with the red phonograph.

Perhaps the most extraordinary difference between my life on Eastville Avenue and one that I would have experienced in Montevetuso was its stunning panorama. On a clear day, gazing eastward, the eye reaches as far as the Gulf of Taranto, on the Ionian Sea. At night, the row of lights on the esplanade might be seen. As a child, I would have become accustomed to this extraordinary vista, which would probably have a lasting impression on my mind, even in a later immigration to a flat city block, as, for example, Eastville Avenue, where the land was organized into block after block.

But beyond the physical configuration of the territory and within my mind, there would have been an indescribable feeling, a depth of emotion within me, for the panorama of that Southern Italian hill city filled with history was haunted by antiquity. Looking far, far out over the silent scrubby landscape, one could imagine the thudding of hooves as civilization after civilization made its way to Montevetuso. In its aim to conquer Southern Italy, each civilization rose and fell, leaving its architectural imprint: Greek sepulchers and vases in red or black; Roman arches; Norman walls, parapets, and mullioned windows on the square campanile of the abbey. Although inevitably fallen, these elements were always there, imbuing the landscape with ghostly essences. Even to this day, traveling to Montevetuso by automobile along curving roads seemingly leading nowhere until, suddenly, far off on a mountain top, one sees ghostly structures. One would think, Oh look! Ruins of an ancient city! Those vistas, those fallen civilizations, that architecture make up that hallowed quality of Montevetuso, a melding of antiquity, the pagan world, and the modern world, today, part of the world of technology.

24

Eastville Avenue at Twilight

It is a summer evening on Eastville Avenue, far, far from Montevetuso. Papa is playing his signature nocturne, Chopin's posthumous Nocturne in E Minor, and Luigi is on a ladder, inspecting the wide-open, flowered faces of his dahlias. But, of course, they are not there, for they are gone.

    The children, my playmates, are making their way to the end of the spacious block, the stretch with no houses, bordered on one side by the sumac woods and on the opposite side by the grassy, treeless lot. But they are no longer children, rushing joyfully up to the game site. They are adults, making their way slowly up the block, and they are old. I recognize them. One or two, Judy and Lila, are walking with canes; Anthony, known for his athleticism, is painfully maneuvering the wheels of his wheelchair as he follows Judy and Lila. Claudette, our daydreaming friend, who wanted to become a Hollywood actress, is wearing a black dress, walking slowly, her head held high, as if she, though now dying, was a princess walking bravely to her fate. And there is my dear, dear friend, Helina, succumbing to cancer, looking around at the city block that nurtured her one last time.

On the topmost step of the stoop of the last house, the one on the right side near the grassy lot, sits the paralyzed man, Mr. Siegle, holding the large white handkerchief in his trembling right hand, to catch the continual trickle of saliva issuing from his mouth. His head is turned toward the children at the game site, and his eyes are filled with something ineffable, something that transcends his tragic fate, leaving an indelible impression upon these pages.

My childhood friends have now reached the curb of the game site and stand there waiting. In the middle of the street is *It*, now, not the red rover caller, but destiny, an amorphous figure, perhaps with large wings, the Angel of Death, perhaps with a chiton, Atropos, one of the three Fates, the cutter of the thread of destiny.

And one by one, they are called over to that other curb and walk slowly on, past the sumac woods. Past time and space.

Darkness falls on Eastville Avenue.

Acknowledgments

I am grateful to Tara Mitchell for reorganizing my chapters and shaping *The Vanishing Generation* into a cohesive whole. I am grateful to graphic designer Sean Mitchell for a book cover design handsomely inviting readers into the that long-ago Bronx and the Third Avenue El. I am grateful to Brian Mitchell for his suggestions and support.

Sources for *The Vanishing Generation* were *The WPA Guide to New York City*, an engaging account of the five boroughs of New York City, with ample illustrations; *Don't You Know There's a War On? The American Home Front, 1941-1945,* By Richard R. Lingeman; *La Storia: Five Centuries of the Italian American Experience,* by Jerre Mangione & Ben Morreale. My primary sources were wartime editions (1945) of newspapers I saved: *The Home News: Bronx and Manhattan;* the New York *Journal American*; the New York *Daily News*.

Acknowledgments

I am grateful to Tara Mitchell for reorganizing my chapters and shaping *The Vanishing Generation* into a cohesive whole. I am grateful to graphic designer Sean Mitchell for a book cover design handsomely inviting readers into the that long-ago Bronx and the Third Avenue El. I am grateful to Brian Mitchell for his suggestions and support.

Sources for *The Vanishing Generation* were *The WPA Guide to New York City*, an engaging account of the five boroughs of New York City, with ample illustrations; *Don't You Know There's a War On? The American Home Front, 1941-1945,* By Richard R. Lingeman; *La Storia: Five Centuries of the Italian American Experience,* by Jerre Mangione & Ben Morreale. My primary sources were wartime editions (1945) of newspapers I saved: *The Home News: Bronx and Manhattan;* the New York *Journal American*; the New York *Daily News.*

About the Author

Irene Musillo Mitchell was born in Basilicata, Italy. She graduated from Hunter College with a music major and received a Master's degree in musicology from Columbia University. Her publications span several literary genres, including poetry and short stories. Her novel *Anna Marilena's Four Sorrows* is set in Italy. Touching upon Italian literature, she wrote *Beatrice Cenci,* a biography, and *Isabella Morra,* a monograph of Renaissance poet, Isabella di Morra, which includes a translation of her poems. She also translated the headnotes for the American English edition of *Italoamericana,* published by Fordham University Press, in 2014. In 2017, she published her latest volume of poems, *A Rim of Lights.*

Printed in the USA
CPSIA information can be obtained
at www.ICGtesting.com
CBHW031158050724
11009CB00003B/260

9 798869 103895